PACK BOOK OF

WASHINGTON, DC

The Essential Guide to America's Capital

HARRIET EDLESON

MAPS BY DAVID LINDROTH

ILLUSTRATED BY
KERREN BARBAS STECKLER

PETER PAUPER PRESS, INC.
WHITE PLAINS, NEW YORK

FOR JACK L. EDLESON,
MY BELOVED FATHER

Illustrations copyright © 2007 Kerren Barbas Steckler
Transportation map copyright © Washington Metropolitan
Area Transit Authority (WMATA)
Neighborhood maps © 2007 David Lindroth, Inc.

Designed by Heather Zschock

Copyright © 2007
Peter Pauper Press, Inc.
202 Mamaroneck Avenue
White Plains, NY 10601
All rights reserved
ISBN 978-1-59359-868-6
Printed in Hong Kong
7 6 5 4 3

Visit us at www.peterpauper.com

THE LITTLE
BLACK BOOK OF

WASHINGTON, DC

CONTENTS

INTRODUCTION

A city of living history, Washington, DC, is home to the U.S. President and Congress, the capital of the largest democratic nation in the world, and the only city established by the U.S. Constitution. But Washington is more than that. It is one of the most vibrant, diverse, and beautiful cities in the U.S. and the world. Dotted with parks and plazas, monuments and memorials, Washington, DC, takes its name from two places: "Washington" from President Washington, and "District of Columbia" from Christopher Columbus. Based on the vision of French engineer-turned-American-soldier Pierre Charles L'Enfant, Washington boasts all the beauty of a European city—diagonal boulevards, parks and gardens, and the grandeur of giant but not towering edifices.

Because no building is more than 20 feet taller than the width of the street or avenue it faces, light pours into the capital city, creating a bright, exciting backdrop for momentous decisions and the daily life of its more than half a million people. Combined with its Maryland and Virginia suburbs, close to four million people live and work in the region.

Washington, DC, is not part of any state, but, at first, was a diamond-shaped city—100 square miles—carved from parts of Maryland and Virginia. In 1846, Congress returned some 30 square miles to Virginia. Beyond the city limits lies the Beltway, Interstate 495, a roadway that encircles Washington's closest suburbs in Maryland and Virginia. Situated midway along the East Coast, it is 90 miles inland from the Atlantic Ocean and 233 miles south of New York City. It's comprised of four quadrants—NW, SW, NE, and SE—that meet at the U.S. Capitol.

Washington, DC, is a city built on compromise. In the beginning, Thomas Jefferson and the southern states sought to situate the new capital city near the southern agricultural region. Alexander Hamilton and the northern states wanted the new nation to absorb Revolutionary War debt. In the end, both got what they wanted.

George Washington chose the precise spot for the new capital on the northern bank of the Potomac River, not far from his Virginia home across the river at Mount Vernon.

The "horse trading" that characterizes the city's origins continues today on Capitol Hill. When disagreements arise, debates erupt, filibusters ensue, and deals are struck.

Washington is two cities. The first is the official city and seat of the federal government that includes the White House and departments of the executive branch; the U.S. Capitol where the House and Senate meet; and the

U.S. Supreme Court, the highest court in the land. The other is the city of neighborhoods and suburbs where many federal workers live and play.

The best way to see Washington is on foot. To grasp the essence of the official city, visit the White House, the major memorials and monuments, and the National Mall, home to the Smithsonian Institution and its collection of museums. Explore its neighborhoods. Enjoy the many free museums, concerts, and outdoor festivals. Indulge in traditional and international-style eateries and stylish restaurants.

GETTING AROUND WASHINGTON

Washington is a relatively easy place to navigate. Visitors can choose from a variety of forms of transportation to reach every area of the city, as well as the Virginia and Maryland suburbs.

Washingtonians tend to be well-informed people, so whether you are using the Metro, Metrobus, or DC Circulator bus, ask questions when traveling. You won't be disappointed. Remember, this is a government town where information is the main industry. Pick up a Metro map at any Metro stop. You also can find Metrobus route maps that connect to that Metro station there.

The Metrorail system, the first segment of which opened in 1976, helped transform the nation's capital into an international center. What began as the Red Line, running from the Metro Center in downtown Washington in a U-shape to the  Maryland suburbs, has spread out into an extensive network of underground rail transportation on the Blue, Orange, Yellow, and, most recently, completion of the Green Line. The Washington Metro is arguably the cleanest, quietest underground rail system in the world. If your hotel is situated near a Metro stop, by all means hop on the Metro and glide to your destination. Purchase a SmarTrip for travel on both Metrorail and Metrobus. Fares are subtracted automatically. Regular and SmarTrip fare cards can be purchased at Metro rail stations throughout the city, and fares are deducted from the card upon exiting. Route maps are posted at every station and inside each Metro car. Each train displays the name of its final destination. *(See the Metro map at the end of this book.)*

A warning regarding mass transit: Washington is not a 24-hour city. Metrorail opens at 5:00 AM weekdays and 7:00 AM weekends, but shuts down at midnight Sunday–Thursday. It stays open until 3:00 AM Friday and Saturday.

The Metro system is linked to the Metrobus system for which a transfer can be obtained at Metro stations before you board the train. Ask the driver for a paper transfer; it's good for two hours for a free ride on the

Metrobus. If you are in less of a hurry and want to see the sights while you travel, try the Metrobus, or pick up one of the newer DC Circulator buses for just a dollar. (The fare is 35 cents with Metro transfer.) It has three routes: between Union Station and Georgetown; between the southwest waterfront and the Washington Convention Center; and a new route recently added that serves major museums and monuments around the Mall. Hours of operation are 7:00 AM to 9:00 PM.

Schedules for the buses on the Metrobus system vary from bus to bus. Contact 202-637-7000 or visit www.metroopensdoors.com to check information for a particular route.

GETTING TO WASHINGTON

Three airports serve the city: Ronald Reagan National Airport, Dulles International Airport, and Baltimore/Washington International Airport. Ronald Reagan National Airport (DCA), referred to as National Airport *(703-417-1818, www.mwaa.com)*, is situated south of the city along the Potomac River, just 15 minutes from downtown and Capitol Hill. If you are planning to stay downtown, in Georgetown, or even in upper Northwest, it's the most convenient way to arrive. Domestic flights on major, regional, and commuter airlines fly into National, and it affords easy access to the city's Metrorail's Blue and Yellow Lines. SuperShuttle *(703-416-7873, 800-BLUEVAN, www.supershuttle.com)* offers shared ride van service.

Dulles Airport (IAD) *(703-572-2700, www.mwaa.com)* is located in Virginia, 26 miles west of the city. A variety of domestic and international carriers fly into Dulles. Otherwise, take the Washington Flyer bus *(Washington Dulles International Airport, 703-685-1400)* to the West Falls Church Metro station (Orange Line); it leaves every 30 minutes.

Baltimore/Washington International Airport (BWI) *(301-261-1000, 800-FLY-FLYI, www.bwiairport.com)* is another option, located 30 miles from Washington. Both domestic and international flights arrive here, but taxi fare to the city can be as high as $45. The MARC train and Amtrak serve BWI Rail Station where free shuttles take you to the airport terminal. BWI Express Metrobus runs between BWI and the Greenbelt Metro station (Green Line) every 40 minutes. Another option, of course, is to rent a car. If you're arriving from New York City, Amtrak *(800-USARAIL, www.amtrak.com)* runs intercity and high-speed trains between New York's Penn Station and Washington's Union Station. Another option is Washington Deluxe *(866-287-6932)*, a motor coach service that runs between the two cities.

HOW TO USE THIS GUIDE

We have included a fold-out map with each chapter to provide a neighborhood-by-neighborhood guide to the city. Color-coded keys help you find on the maps the places mentioned in the text. **Red** symbols indicate **Places to See**, including landmarks, arts & entertainment, and activities for children. **Blue** symbols indicate **Places to Eat & Drink**, which include restaurants, cafés, and nightspots. **Orange** symbols indicate **Where to Shop**. Finally, **Green** symbols show **Where to Stay**.

Below are our keys for restaurant and hotel prices:

Restaurants
Price of an appetizer and main course without drinks
($) Up to $25
($$) $25 to $45
($$$) $45 and up

Hotels
Price per night
($) $50 to $125
($$) $125 to $250
($$$) $250 and up

MORE TIPS FOR VISITORS

The **Washington, DC Convention & Tourism Corporation** *(901 7th St. NW, 4th fl., 202-789-7000 or 800-635-MEET, www.washington.org)* is a comprehensive information source for visitors. Contact them for up-to-the-minute hotel availability. The **DC Visitor Information Center,** run by the Chamber of Commerce, *(1300 Pennsylvania Ave. NW, in the Ronald Reagan Building, www.DCChamber.org)* is another good source of visitor information. Want to catch a show while you're in town? **TicketPlace** *(407 Seventh St. NW, between D and E Sts., 202-842-5387, www.ticketplace.org)* sells half-price, day-of and advance tickets. Credit or debit card only, no cash or checks.

SEASONAL EVENTS

Winter–Spring:

National Christmas Tree Lighting, December *(Ellipse south of the White House; tickets required for every attendee, including children; the National Park Service distributes free tickets at Ellipse Visitor Pavilion, southwest corner of 15th and E Sts.; maximum of four tickets per person; 202-208-1631, www.pageantofpeace.org)*.

Illumination of National Christmas Tree and Pathway of Peace, nightly, dusk-11:00 PM from the date of the National Tree Lighting–January 1; 56 small trees representing the 50 states, five territories, and the District of Columbia—the Pathway of Peace—surround the National Christmas Tree; musical entertainment each evening *(Ellipse south of the White House, 202-208-1631, www.pageantofpeace.org).*

 Lighting of the National Menorah, December, lighting of the world's largest Menorah to mark the eight-day festival of Chanukah *(northwest end of the Ellipse near Constitution Ave., tickets required, 202-332-5600, www. nps.gov/ncro/PublicAffairs/YearlyCalendar.html).*

National Cherry Blossom Festival, March–April, a celebration of spring and the 1912 gift of 3,000 pink-and-white blossoming cherry trees from the city of Tokyo *(Tidal Basin surrounding Jefferson Memorial and city-wide, 202-547-1500, www.nationalcherryblossomfestival.org).*

Smithsonian Kite Festival, late March, with competitions, displays, and activities for all ages *(National Mall, 202-357-3030, www.kitefestival.org).*

White House Easter Egg Roll, first Monday after Easter *(White House South Lawn; tickets required; the National Park Service distributes free tickets at The Ellipse Visitor Pavilion, southwest corner of 15th and E Sts., 202-456-7041, www.whitehouse.gov/easter).*

National Memorial Day Parade, Memorial Day, free event honoring U.S. veterans *(202-777-7272 ext. 220, www.nationalmemorialdayparade.com).*

Summer:

Capital Pride, June, fourth largest gay pride event in the U.S.; includes live entertainment, parade, and street festival *(202-797-3510, www.capitalpride.org)*.

Independence Day, July 4, with a noon-time National Parade along Constitution Ave., an evening concert by the National Symphony, and one of the country's largest fireworks displays *(800-215-6405, www.july4thparade. com or www.nps.gov/ncro/PublicAffairs/ Independenceday.htm)*.

The Smithsonian Folklife Festival, June–July, celebration of international living traditions with day and evening programs of music, song, dance, crafts, cooking, storytelling, and more *(National Mall, 202-275-1150, www.folklife.si.edu/center/festival.html)*.

Twilight Tattoo, every Wednesday at 7:00 PM from mid-April–July; sunset military pageant performed by members of the 3rd U.S. Infantry (The Old Guard), the U.S. Army Band "Pershing's Own," the Fife and Drum Corps, and the U.S. Army Drill Team; bleacher seating on a first-come, first-served basis *(Ellipse near the White House, 202-685-2888)*.

Autumn:

Black Family Reunion Celebration, September, said to be the largest family event in the nation; two-day celebration of the African American family; features live music, ethnic foods, and arts and crafts *(National Mall; reunion is free; opening ceremony and prayer breakfast tickets can be purchased by calling 202-737-0120, www.ncnw.org/events/reunion)*.

Adams Morgan Day, 2nd Sunday in September, popular DC festival fetes the international character and famous murals of the Adams Morgan neighborhood; live music, international food, colorful vendors, cultural demonstrations, and kids' fair *(202-232-1960, www.ammainstreet.org)*.

National Book Festival, September, free festival features authors, illustrators, and poets; sponsored by the Library of Congress *(National Mall, 888-714-4696, www.loc.gov/bookfest)*.

Veterans Day, November 11, U.S. veterans are honored with wreath-laying ceremonies, speeches, storytelling, and other commemorations at memorials throughout Washington, DC, including Arlington National Cemetery, the African-American Civil War Memorial, the U.S. Navy Memorial, and the Vietnam Veterans Memorial *(202-619-7222, nps.gov/ncro)*.

WASHINGTON, DC'S TOP PICKS

TOP PICK!

Washington offers an abundance of one-of-a-kind attractions and experiences for visitors. Here are 15 of the top picks, not to be missed!

- ★ **White House** *(see page 22)*
- ★ **Washington Monument** *(see page 25)*
- ★ **National World War II Memorial** *(see page 27)*
- ★ **Vietnam Veterans Memorial** *(see page 29)*
- ★ **Lincoln Memorial** *(see page 30)*
- ★ **Franklin Delano Roosevelt Memorial** *(see page 32)*
- ★ **Thomas Jefferson Memorial** *(see page 33)*
- ★ **U.S. Holocaust Memorial Museum** *(see page 34)*
- ★ **National Air and Space Museum** *(see page 55)*
- ★ **U.S. Capitol Building** *(see page 62)*
- ★ **Supreme Court of the United States** *(see page 65)*
- ★ **Library of Congress** *(see page 68)*
- ★ **National Archives Building** *(see page 103)*
- ★ **National Portrait Gallery/Smithsonian American Art Museum** *(see page 107)*
- ★ **Washington National Cathedral** *(see page 123)*

chapter 1

THE WHITE HOUSE AND
THE MONUMENTS

LAFAYETTE SQUARE
AND ENVIRONS

THE WHITE HOUSE AND THE MONUMENTS
LAFAYETTE SQUARE AND ENVIRONS

Places to See:

1. WHITE HOUSE ★
2. White House Visitor Center
3. Dwight D. Eisenhower Executive Office Building
4. U.S. Treasury Building
5. President's Park and the Ellipse
6. WASHINGTON MONUMENT ★
7. NATIONAL WORLD WAR II MEMORIAL ★
8. Reflecting Pool
9. Constitution Gardens
10. VIETNAM VETERANS MEMORIAL ★
11. LINCOLN MEMORIAL ★
12. Korean War Veterans Memorial
13. Tidal Basin
14. DC World War I Memorial
15. FRANKLIN DELANO ROOSEVELT MEMORIAL ★
16. THOMAS JEFFERSON MEMORIAL ★
17. U.S. HOLOCAUST MEMORIAL MUSEUM ★
18. Bureau of Engraving and Printing
19. National Aquarium
36. St. John's Episcopal Church
37. Equestrian Statue of President Andrew Jackson
38. Statue of Lafayette
39. Blair House
40. Decatur House
41. Octagon House
42. Renwick Gallery of the Smithsonian American Art Museum
43. Corcoran Gallery of Art
44. American Red Cross Visitors Center
45. Daughters of the American Revolution Museum
46. DAR Constitution Hall
47. Art Museum of the Americas

★ *Top Picks*

Places to Eat & Drink:

20. Café 1401
21. Willard Room
22. Sky Terrace
23. Butterfield 9
24. Avenue Grill at the JW Marriott
25. Corner Bakery Café
26. Potbelly Sandwich Works
27. Red Sage
28. Old Ebbitt Grill
29. U.S. Holocaust Memorial Museum Café
48. Loeb's Deli Restaurant
49. Eye Street Grille
50. Café 15
51. The Oval Room
52. Georgia Brown's
53. Caribou Coffee
54. Taberna del Alabardero

Where to Shop:

30. The Shops at National Place/National Press Building:
    Political Americana
    The White House Gift Shop
    Filene's Basement
31. Greenworks
32. Chas Schwartz & Son Jewelers

Where to Stay:

33. Willard InterContinental Washington
34. Hotel Washington
35. JW Marriott
55. Hay-Adams Hotel
56. The St. Regis Washington, DC
57. Sofitel Lafayette Square

How prophetic L'Enfant was when he laid out Washington as a city that goes around in circles!

—John Mason Brown

⬤⬤ *to Foggy Bottom/GWU, or Farragut West,
or McPherson Square, or Metro Center,
or Federal Triangle, or Smithsonian*

⬤ *to Metro Center*

• SNAPSHOT •

The White House, official home and office of the president of the United States, and its surrounding green spaces and historical monuments evoke a strong sense of national power and history, and are vivid reminders of those who shaped America's earliest days and those who made sacrifices for the country since its turbulent beginning. Spending time at each is a real-life, hands-on way to learn American history without opening a book. You may want to time your visit to coincide with the National Cherry Blossom Festival in late March/early April when the Tidal Basin is engulfed in a cloud of pale and dark pink cherry blossoms. Check the map at the beginning of this chapter if you have a specific landmark in mind and see which Metro stops brings you closest to it. However, the best way to explore DC is on foot, so don your most comfortable shoes and get going!

PLACES TO SEE
Landmarks:

The ★**WHITE HOUSE (1)** *(1600 Pennsylvania Ave. NW, 202-456-2200, www.whitehouse.gov/)* is probably the most recognizable building in Washington, DC, with its distinctive design by Irish-born architect James Hoban. The cornerstone was laid in 1782, and the building was finished in time for the second U.S. President, John Adams, and his wife Abigail to become the first official residents in 1800. During the War of 1812, the British torched the house, gutting the interior, but a summer thunderstorm saved the exterior from destruction. President James Madison brought Hoban back to restore the structure; after three years it was ready for occupancy. The sandstone mansion was again painted white, and Theodore Roosevelt had "The White House" engraved on his official stationery in 1901, giving it the name that has endured ever since.

TOP PICK!

Few people realize how large the structure actually is. It has six stories with 132 rooms, 35 bathrooms, 28 fireplaces, a tennis court, a bowling alley, a movie theater, jogging track, and a swimming pool. In 1961, Jacqueline Kennedy, wife of the 35th president, formed a fine arts committee to restore the landmark's well-worn furnishings to their original grandeur. Because of her efforts, the **White House (1)** now enjoys a museum-like collection of

antiques. A few of the public rooms are open to visitors, including the white-and-gold East Room (used for press conferences), the Green Room (used for photo shoots), and the State Dining Room, which seats 140 people.

More than 80 types of trees planted over the years by every presidential family thrive in the surrounding 18 acres. The famous Rose Garden was planted in 1913. The grounds are closed to visitors except during the Easter Egg Roll and Garden Tours.

Free **White House (1)** tours are currently available for parties of 10 or more people. Tour requests must be submitted through your Member of Congress *(www.house.gov)*, are accepted up to six months in advance, and are scheduled about one month in advance of your requested date. Keep in mind that tours are subject to last-minute cancellation. For the most current information, call the 24-hour line: 202-456-7041.

About a block away, the **White House Visitor Center (2)** *(14th St. and Constitution Ave. NW, 202-208-1631)* offers permanent exhibits relating to the **White House (1)** and its furnishings, first families, and ceremonies. Royal gifts are also on display.

Next, head to the **Dwight D. Eisenhower Executive Office Building (3)** *(Pennsylvania and 17th St. NW, 202-395-5895, www.whitehouse.gov/history/eeobtour)*. Also known as the Old Executive Office Building, it was built between 1871 and 1888, and remains a major example of French Second Empire architecture. Formerly the State, War, and Navy Department Building, and once the largest office building in Washington, its granite walls exude power. You're likely to see all the president's men and women—executive branch staffers—rushing in and out. Tours used to be conducted on Saturdays, but have currently been suspended.

On the grounds to the south, look skyward to see the **First Division War Memorial**. It's a tribute to the some 5,500 U.S. soldiers who lost their lives in World War I. Created by Daniel Chester French, its gilded bronze Winged Victory stands atop the striking 78-foot marble column, forming an impressive silhouette against the sky.

The massive Greek Revival building next to the White House on the other side is the **U.S. Treasury Building (4)** *(1500 Pennsylvania Ave. NW, 202-622-0896, www. ustreas.gov)*. This is where Andrew Johnson's temporary office was located after Lincoln's assassination. Outside is a statue of Alexander Hamilton, the department's first secretary. Tours have been suspended indefinitely.

Just south of the White House and the Treasury Building is **President's Park (5)** *(the White House grounds)* and the **Ellipse (5)**, once used for sheep and cattle grazing when it was undeveloped marshland before the 1860s. The northern edge of the park is where the national Christmas tree is displayed.

TOP PICK!

As you continue walking south, you'll see the ★**WASHINGTON MONUMENT (6)** *(15th St. and Constitution Ave. NW, 202-426-6841, www.nps.gov/wamo)*. The 555-foot, white-marble obelisk is an imposing silhouette (it's the tallest building in DC). The monument was designed by Robert Mills and the cornerstone laid in 1848, but controversy (a commemorative stone donated by Pope Pius IX was stolen by anti-papists), lack of funds, and the Civil War

halted construction on it for more than 10 years. You can see how far the initial builders got by the change of color in the stone about 150 feet up. Construction resumed in 1876 and was completed in 1884, when the monument's marble capstone was set, topped with a 9-inch aluminum tip, and wired with lightning conductors. Officially opened to the public in 1888, the **Washington Monument (6)** made a fitting memorial to founding father George Washington, first president of the United States.

The interior (made of Maine granite) features nearly 200 commemorative stones donated by U.S. states, other nations, groups, and individuals. Inserted among the granite blocks, these include stones donated by the Cherokee Nation; the New York City Fire Department; the Sultan of Turkey; the Ladies of Lowell, Massachusetts; numerous Masonic groups, and the State of Alaska, which contributed a stone of pure jade. The **Washington Monument (6)** officially opened to the public in 1888.

An iron stairway consisting of 897 steps and 50 landings leads to the observation tower, but visitors are no longer permitted to climb them. Instead, you can ride the elevator 50 stories to the top (it takes about one minute), where the 360-degree views of DC, Virginia, and Maryland are breathtaking. Fifty flags, representing each state, surround the monument's base. Individual same-day tickets are free on a first-come, first-served basis at a kiosk at the base of the monument on 15th Street NW beginning at 8 AM. However, they do run out early. To purchase advance tickets, call 800-967-2283 or visit reservations.nps.gov.

Several other significant monuments are clustered together between 17th and 23rd Streets NW and between Constitution and Independence Avenues NW.

In 1987, Roger Durbin of Ohio, a former Army tank mechanic under General George Patton, asked his Representative, Marcy Kaptur, if a World War II memorial could be built. She introduced legislation in 1987, and again in 1989, 1991, and 1993. Finally, Congress passed legislation authorizing the building of a National World War II Memorial in Washington, DC or its immediate environs; it was signed into law by President Clinton on May 25, 1993. An advisory board that included Senator Bob Dole was appointed to oversee site selection and fund-raising. A design by Friedrich

St. Florian of Rhode Island was selected in a competition that attracted more than 400 entries. Eleven years later, on May 29, 2004, President George W. Bush dedicated the ★NATIONAL WORLD WAR II MEMORIAL (7) *(east end of the Reflecting Pool, between the Lincoln Memorial and the Washington Monument, www.wwiimemorial.com)* in a ceremony that drew 150,000, including Tom Hanks, Tom Brokaw, and scores of WWII veterans and their families. (Sadly, Roger Durbin had passed away in 2000, but his grandchildren were honored guests.)

TOP PICK!

Now one of DC's most popular sights, the 7-1/2-acre memorial, with its plaza, Freedom Wall, and Rainbow Pool, is a powerful tribute to the "Greatest Generation," the 16 million American men and women who served in the Great War, and the more than 400,000 who perished. Curved ramps provide access to the plaza for visitors walking along the east-west pathways between the Lincoln Memorial and Washington Monument. The 17th Street ceremonial entrance is flanked by two flagpoles. Two baldachinos, or stone canopies, mark the north and south plaza entries; they feature four bronze columns with four American eagles bearing a laurel wreath, a symbol of victory. Sit along the circumference of the 246-foot Rainbow Pool and enjoy its waterworks, along with the memorial's other fountains and waterfalls; they're intended to evoke a celebratory note.

Fifty-six granite pillars, connected by a sculpted rope of bronze, symbolize each U.S. state and territory. Scenes on 24 bas-relief panels by sculptor Raymond Kaskey, and based on archival photographs, trace the war on Atlantic and Pacific fronts. From Pearl Harbor, enlistment, shipbuilding, and Rosie the Riveter, to tanks in combat, the Navy in action, the Normandy Beach Landing, and liberation, the story of America's transformation and unity of purpose unfolds. Visitors will also be delighted by the "Kilroy Was Here" graffiti engraved on the memorial; the cartoon figure "Kilroy" turned up on every front during WWII, confounding enemies and rallying U.S. troops.

Finally, the Freedom Wall on the western side of the memorial, with its field of 4,000 sculpted gold stars (one for approximately 100 American deaths during the war), is accompanied by the inscription, "Here we mark the price of freedom." The northwestern corner of the memorial site offers a landscaped contemplative area.

The memorial, which is especially dramatic when illuminated at night, is open daily except Christmas.

Stroll by the **Reflecting Pool (8)** *(between the Washington Monument and Lincoln Memorial)*, an elongated rectangle so-named because it reflects the **Washington Monument (6)** at night, and relax in **Constitution Gardens (9)** *(north of the Reflecting Pool, 202-619-7222, www. nps.gov/coga)*, 45 acres of landscaped grounds, including a small lake and an island that were originally under the Potomac River. Trees and benches line the paths, creating a great place to picnic.

The haunting ★VIETNAM VETERANS MEMORIAL (10) *(Bacon Dr. and Constitution Ave., 202-426-6841, www.nps.gov/vive)* honors members of the U.S. armed forces lost in America's longest, and one of its most controversial, conflicts. The black granite "V" wall lists nearly 60,000 names of those killed, missing in action, or held as prisoners of war; the names are listed in chronological order, the first dating from 1959. The memorial was conceived by the Vietnam Veterans Memorial Fund organization to make no political statement about the war; instead, its purpose is to encourage reconciliation and healing. A national competition for the memorial's design was announced in 1980; 1,421 entries were received. Number 1,026, submitted by 21-year-old Yale student Maya Ying Lin, was chosen. But Lin's stark, below-ground-level design proved as divisive as the conflict it was based on, and prolonged debate placed the Fund in danger of losing its two-acre memorial site. At last, a compromise was decided—the site would include a 60-foot flagpole and two sculptures. The life-size **Three Servicemen Statue**, with its trio of battle-worn soldiers, represents camaraderie and reconciliation. The **Vietnam Women's Memorial**, a tribute to the

TOP PICK!

women who served, portrays three uniformed women aiding a wounded male soldier. The eight trees around the plaza commemorate each of the women in the military who died in Vietnam.

TOP PICK! A brief walk southwest will take you to the ★**LINCOLN MEMORIAL (11)** *(23rd St. and Constitution Ave. NW, 202-426-6841, www.nps.gov/linc),* honoring the 16th president. Planning for this memorial began in 1867, two years after Lincoln's death. A symbol of American democracy and freedom, it also memorializes the conclusion of the American Civil War. Designed by Henry Bacon in 1912, and modeled after the ancient Greek Parthenon in Athens, the memorial is particularly

compelling at dawn or dusk. Its 36 Doric columns represent the states in the Union at the time of Lincoln's death. Inside the memorial is the colossal, 19-foot-high seated statue of Lincoln. Called by some "The Brooding Lincoln," this famous sculpture designed by Daniel Chester French, weighs 175 tons. It was carved from 28 blocks of white Georgian marble. As you approach the monument, the figure seems to disappear; as you climb the stairs, Lincoln majestically comes into view. The monument's chamber is composed of limestone walls inscribed with the Gettysburg Address and Lincoln's Second Inaugural Address.

The memorial to the "Great Emancipator" is also the

site of historic gatherings. In 1939, the Daughters of the American Revolution refused to allow internationally renowned African-American singer Marian Anderson to perform at their Constitution Hall (an action that prompted First Lady Eleanor Roosevelt to resign from the organization). With the assistance of Mrs. Roosevelt and the "Committee for Marian Anderson," Anderson instead performed at the **Lincoln Memorial (11)** to an audience of more than 70,000. (The D.A.R. finally invited Marian to perform for a war relief concert in 1943.)

Twenty-four years later, Martin Luther King, Jr. delivered his unforgettable "I Have a Dream" speech here after a civil rights march. Look for the words "I Have a Dream. Martin Luther King, Jr., The March on Washington for Jobs and Freedom, August 28, 1963," inscribed on the granite steps; they mark the spot where Dr. King stood.

To the southeast, you'll see the **Korean War Veterans Memorial (12)** *(West Potomac Park, Independence Ave. next to the Lincoln Memorial, 202-426-6841, www. nps.kwvm)*, one of the newer monuments in the area; it was dedicated in 1995 and features 19 statues of soldiers by sculptor Frank Gaylord, their weary faces reflecting the harsh realities of the war.

On a bright note, head further southeast to one of the most picturesque spots in the Capital City, the **Tidal Basin (13)** *(West Basin Drive)*. Encircled by more than 3,000 cherry trees—a 1912 gift from the people of

Japan—it's a local and tourist favorite. Rent a paddleboat for a close-up view of the blossoms in early spring. Musicians and dancers perform on the Tidal Basin stage here during the annual Cherry Blossom Festival in late March/early April.

A brief walk northwest of the **Tidal Basin (13)** will take you to the **DC World War I Memorial (14)** *(east of the Reflecting Pool, north of Independence Ave.)*, a dome over a circle of Doric columns. Dating from 1931, it commemorates local heroes of the First World War.

TOP PICK! To get to the popular 7-1/2 acre **★FRANKLIN DELANO ROOSEVELT MEMORIAL (15)** *(1850 W. Basin Dr. SW, 202-426-6841, www.nps.gov/fdrm)*, walk directly south toward the Potomac River. Dedicated in 1997, the FDR memorial is a tribute to the "People's President" who led the U.S. through some of its most trying times, from the Great Depression to WWII. Four outdoor galleries, arranged chronologically, depict scenes from the 32nd president's unprecedented four terms in office, featuring the New Deal, fireside chats, the attack on Pearl Harbor, and the public's shock at Roosevelt's passing at age 63, just months after his fourth inaugural.

The memorial incorporates bronze statues of FDR, and one of First Lady Eleanor Roosevelt, as well as shade trees, reflecting pools, and waterfalls. Quotations by

FDR are engraved into walls of red South Dakota granite. This was the first DC memorial specifically designed to be wheelchair-accessible; you'll see a statue of the president in his wheelchair at the front of the memorial, which is located along Cherry Tree Walk on the western edge of the Tidal Basin.

Note: You'll find a much smaller memorial to Roosevelt at 9th Street and Pennsylvania Avenue on the grounds of the National Archives. The president reportedly once said that a desk-sized block of stone placed at the Archives would suffice as his memorial. A simple marble slab was installed there in the 1960s to fulfill that original request; engraved upon it are the words, "In Memory of Franklin Delano Roosevelt 1882–1945."

Southeast of the Tidal Basin in East Potomac Park, the 2-1/2 acre ★**THOMAS JEFFERSON MEMORIAL (16)** *(Tidal Basin South End, East Basin Dr. SW, 202-426-6841, www.nps.gov/thje)* commemorates the third U.S. President. Franklin Delano Roosevelt, who spearheaded the memorial's construction, laid the cornerstone in 1939. Designed by John Russell Pope, the open-air, marble structure emulates the classical style favored by Jefferson and resembles his own Monticello.

TOP PICK!

It was dedicated on April 13, 1943, the 200th anniversary of Jefferson's birth.

Outside the memorial,

above the entrance, you'll see a sculpture of Jefferson with Benjamin Franklin, John Adams, Robert Livingston, and Roger Sherman, all of whom composed the Declaration of Independence. Inside, atop a six-foot pedestal of black granite, you'll find a towering, 19-foot bronze statue of Jefferson addressing the Continental Congress, a copy of the Declaration of Independence in his left hand. Sculpted by Virginia artist Rudulph Evans, who studied in France with Auguste Rodin, the statue is clad in a fur cloak given to Jefferson by friend and Revolutionary hero, the Polish general Thaddeus Kosciuszko. (Jefferson once said of Kosciuszko, "As pure a son of liberty as I have ever known.") The statue is surrounded by passages from Jefferson's writings, including the Declaration of Independence. A small museum beneath the monument is devoted to his legacy.

Arts & Entertainment:

TOP PICK!

The ★**U.S. HOLOCAUST MEMORIAL MUSEUM (17)** *(100 Raoul Wallenberg Pl. SW, 202-488-0400, www.ushmm.org)* to the north is America's memorial to the millions of Jews, Poles, Jehovah's Witnesses, Gypsies, homosexuals, political prisoners, mentally and physically disabled people, and others killed by the Nazis between 1933 and 1945. The museum's permanent exhibit, The Holocaust, is divided into three parts: Nazi Assault, Final Solution, and Last Chapter. The tour begins with eyewitness accounts of American soldiers describing what they found during the liberation of the concentration camps at the end of World War II. Each visitor is assigned an identity card of a real person from the Holocaust; throughout the tour, the card provides additional information on that person's status. The Holocaust story is told through more than 900 artifacts (including a Polish freight car like those used to transport Warsaw Jews to the Treblinka death camp), videos, historic film footage, and eyewitness accounts. A second-floor Rescuers' Wall lists the names of those who risked their lives to save Jewish men, women, and children.

The permanent exhibit is not recommended for children under 11 years of age, but those eight and older are invited to the special first-floor exhibition, "Remember the Children: Daniel's Story," an account of the Holocaust as seen through the eyes of an eight-year-old Jewish boy.

Timed-entry passes, available on a first-come, first-served basis at opening time (lines begin forming about 8:00 AM), are necessary to view the permanent exhibit. Passes are not needed for "Daniel's Story," the Wall of Remembrance, a memorial to the 1.5 million children killed during the Holocaust, or the museum's Wexner Learning Center. Advance tickets for the museum are available through www.tickets.com or 800-400-9373.

If you're traveling with children, check out the **Bureau of Engraving and Printing (18)** *(14th and C Sts. SW, 202-874-2330 or 866-874-2330, www.moneyfactory.com)* next door to the **U.S. Holocaust Memorial Museum (17)**. There's a 45-minute tour every 15 minutes Monday–

Friday. Watch the printing, cutting, and stacking of the 37 million bank notes produced daily.

Another place for kids is the **National Aquarium (19)** *(U.S. Commerce Building, 14th St. and Constitution Ave. NW, 202-482-2825, www. national aquarium.com)*, the oldest in the country. It's located in the basement, and though small, can amuse younger children for at least an hour.

PLACES TO EAT & DRINK
Where to Eat:

A mainstay in this area for weekday breakfast and lunch is **Café 1401 (20) ($$)** *(Willard InterContinental Washington, 1401 Pennsylvania Ave. NW, 202-637-7401, www.washington.interconti.com)*. Washington insiders as well as visitors frequent this casual restaurant for business or pleasure. Dine in style at the **Willard Room (21) ($$-$$$)** *(Willard InterContinental Washington, 1401 Pennsylvania Ave. NW, 202-637-7440, www.washington.interconti.com)*, a two-story, oak-paneled, turn-of-the-century restaurant that serves some of the best American and European cuisine in Washington. **Butterfield 9 (23) ($$-$$$)** *(600 14th St. NW, 202-BU9-8810, www.butterfield9.com)* is a Continental restaurant that attracts the power lunch crowd. Large, stylish, black-and-white fashion photographs of the 1930s, 1940s, and 1950s adorn the walls. Try the 3-course pre-/post-theater menu. **Avenue Grill at the JW Marriott (24) ($$–$$$)** *(1331 Pennsylvania Ave.*

NW, 202-626-6970) features classic American food. Opt for the Angus steak and salad. If you want a quick breakfast, lunch, or dinner, eat with the business crowd at the **Corner Bakery Café (25) ($)** *(529 14th St. NW, 202-662-7400, www.cornerbakerycafe.com)*. For American, Southwest, and Nuevo Latino cuisine, try **Red Sage (27) ($$)** *(605 14th St. NW, 202-638-4444, www.redsage.com)*, known for its first-rate food and ambience. If you want a quick bite, and kosher, too, try the **U.S. Holocaust Memorial Museum Café (29) ($)** *(100 Raoul Wallenberg Pl. SW, 202-488-6151)*. You can even pre-order a bag lunch to go if you're in a rush.

Bars & Nightlife:

For drama, check out the **Sky Terrace (22)** *(Hotel Washington, 515 15th St. NW, 202-638-5900, ext. 3140, www.hotelwashington.com)*, where, weather permitting,

you can dine or sip a tropical cocktail on an open-air roof terrace offering panoramic views of the Mall, monuments, and the White House. Not to be missed is the **Old Ebbitt Grill (28)** *(675 15th St. NW, 202-347-4800, www.ebbitt.com)*, a Washington institution and its oldest bar, dating to 1856. Popular with Presidents Theodore Roosevelt, Cleveland, and Grant, it's still a favorite meeting place for political insiders and celebrities. Make a reservation or be willing to wait for a table in the bar at peak hours. It's worth the wait, however; you won't be disappointed.

WHERE TO SHOP

This area is not a shopping mecca; however, there are a few stores in and around The Shops at National Place/National Press Building (30) *(529 14th St. NW)*. **Political Americana** *(202-737-7730, www.politicalamericana.com)* is the place for collectible souvenirs of Washington. **The White House Gift Shop** *(202-662-7280, www.whitehousegiftshop .com)*, sells glassware, fine pens, notebooks, jewelry, mugs, White House shirts, kids' clothing, and other souvenirs. **Filene's Basement** is also located here.

A collection of gift items, flowers, candles, pottery, decorative arts, and antique furniture makes Greenworks (31) *(1455 Pennsylvania Ave. NW, 202-393-2142)* great for browsing or buying. Need a special gift for your beloved? Chas Schwartz & Son Jewelers (32) *(Willard Intercontinental Washington, 1400 F St. NW, 202-737-4757)* features a collection of high-end diamonds, sapphires, and estate jewelry.

WHERE TO STAY

One of the most renowned hotels in Washington is undoubtedly the Willard InterContinental Washington (33) ($$$) *(1401 Pennsylvania Ave. NW, 202-628-9100 or 800-827-1747, www.washington.interconti.com)*. Designated a National Historic Landmark in 1974, it's noted for its Beaux-Arts elegance and close proximity to the White House and Capitol Hill. Take a look in its imposing hallway lobby, stretching from the 14th and F Street entrance to the main entrance on Pennsylvania Avenue. Lobbyists have packed this spot since the mid-1800s to hash out issues of the day. Check out the exhibit that traces the highlights of life at the Willard, too. Just a block away is the venerable **Hotel Washington (34) ($$-$$$)** *(515 15th St. NW, 202-638-5900 or 800-424-9540, www.hotelwashington.com)*. Its Sky Room and open-air Sky Terrace afford sweeping views of the city below. Closer to the Metro center, **JW Marriott (35) ($$$)** *(1331 Pennsylvania Ave. NW, 202-393-2000 or 800-228-9290, www.jwmarriottdc.com)* is convenient to the White House and the adjacent business district.

●● *to McPherson Square*

● SNAPSHOT ●

If you want to learn about the history and culture of the capital city, you can't miss if you spend some time in Lafayette Square and its surroundings. Gaze at the White House looming in front of you, and imagine past presidents politicking in these very same places. The wide-open, seven-acre green space located between H Street and Pennsylvania Avenue and between 15th and 17th Streets, NW, was once owned by Edward Pearce; his farmhouse was near the northeast corner of the square. An apple orchard and a family burial ground were located here in the late 1600s, but the federal government took title of the land in 1792 when construction of the capital city was underway. Statues of four men from foreign countries who served as generals in

the Revolutionary War mark each of the square's corners: the Marquis de Lafayette, the compte de Rochambeau, Baron von Steuben, and Thaddeus Kosciuszko. In contemporary times, the square is the site of celebrations and protests.

PLACES TO SEE
Landmarks:

Begin your exploration just north of Lafayette Square at **St. John's Episcopal Church (36)** *(16th and H Sts. NW, www.stjohns-dc.org)*, built in 1816 by architect Benjamin Latrobe. With its bright yellow stuccoed walls and golden yellow cupola and dome, it is difficult to miss. Every President since James Madison has worshipped here at some point, traditionally in pew 54. As you walk south, don't miss the striking views of the White House before you. In the center of Lafayette Square stands Clark Mills's **Equestrian Statue of President Andrew Jackson (37)**, erected in 1853.

Stop at the southeast corner of the park to view the **Statue of Lafayette (38)**, turning right and continuing in front of the White House until you reach the **Blair House (39)** *(1651–1653 Pennsylvania Ave. NW)*. Owner Francis Preston Blair (1791–1876) was the founder and editor of the *Washington Globe* from 1830–1845. In the 1940s, the house became the official residence of visiting dignitaries and, during White House remodeling, President Harry S. Truman moved here temporarily. Walk north along the square on Jackson Place to the **Decatur House (40)** *(748 Jackson Pl. NW, 202-842-0920, www.decaturhouse.org, Tuesday–Sunday, entrance at 1610 H St. NW)*, one of the oldest houses in DC. Stop in and hear compelling tales about a slave's fight for freedom and details of a fatal duel. Congressmen, businessmen, politicians, and diplomats chose the address as a residence for its proximity to the White House. As you walk south, you'll see the **Octagon House (41)** *(1799 New York Ave. NW, 202-638-3221, www.archfoundation.org/octagon)*, built for plantation owner John Tayloe III in 1801. President Madison and his wife lived here when the White House was burned in the War of 1812. During the Civil War, General George McClellan used it as his headquarters, and in 1897, during the William McKinley administration, Vice President Garret Augustus Hobart leased it, hence the name, "Little White House." Now it is home to the American Institute of Architects.

Arts & Entertainment:

There is more to Washington than policy and power. When you tire of politics, history, and government, choose among the many museums near Lafayette Square, all within 10–15 minutes of each other. Start at the **Renwick Gallery of the Smithsonian American Art Museum (42)** *(Pennsylvania Avenue at 17th St. NW, 202-633-1000, www.americanart.si.edu, free admission)* for a trip into the world of fine American crafts and decorative arts from the 19th–21st centuries. Be sure to wander through the Grand Salon on the second floor and enjoy the re-creation of a 19th-century collector's picture gallery. Look for *Game Fish*, a colorful collage fashioned from toys and game pieces, such as yo-yos and Scrabble tiles. Walk south on 17th Street for a few minutes and you'll see the **Corcoran Gallery of Art (43)** *(500 17th St. NW, entrance on 17th, New York/E St., 202-639-1700, www.corcoran.org)*, which houses an extensive collection of American master-works and European and contemporary art. Tune into your jazz side and tap your feet to the sounds of the gallery's free jazz concerts every first and third Wednesday of the month. The Corcoran moved to this space, a French Beaux-Arts structure with Greek-inspired details in 1897. Designed by Ernest Flagg, who is also responsible for the U.S. Naval Academy at Annapolis, it houses the **Corcoran College of Art + Design**, which adjoins the gallery.

Drop by the **American Red Cross Visitors Center (44)** *(1730 E St. NW, 202-639-3300, www.redcross.org)* to explore the role of the Red Cross in disaster relief and emergency preparedness. For an early American history lesson, stop at the **Daughters of the American Revolution Museum (45)** *(1776 D St. NW, 202-879-3241, www.dar.org/museum)*, one block south, where you'll tour more than 30 period-decorated rooms. Among them is a one-room Pilgrim century dwelling, a Victorian parlor, a tavern, and an attic filled with toys and dolls. Next door to the museum, **DAR Constitution Hall (46)** *(311 18th St. NW; open to the public during performances)*, a venue for concerts and other performing arts, is the largest auditorium in DC. To view Latin American and Caribbean art, stop at the **Art Museum of** the Americas **(47)** *(201 18th St. NW, 202-458-6016, www.oas.org)*, part of the Organization of American States. Architect Paul Cret designed the Spanish colonial-style building that houses OAS in 1912.

PLACES TO EAT & DRINK
Where to Eat:

For a fun meal, head to **Potbelly Sandwich Works (26) ($)** *(1400 New York Ave. at 14th St. NW, 202-628-9500, www.potbelly.com)*. It seems everyone who works in the neighborhood crowds inside here; it also serves shakes, malts, yogurt smoothies, chili, and soups. **Loeb's Deli Restaurant (48) ($)** *(832 15th St. NW, corner of I, 202-371-1150, www.loebs nydeli.com)* is the kind of informal place that will make you feel at home right away. If you want a deli sandwich or other inexpensive lunch or dinner, this is one of the best bets in the neighborhood. Another choice for a quick lunch while sightseeing is the **Eye Street Grille (49) ($)** *(1575 I St, 15th/16th Sts., 202-289-7561)*, where the salad bar is plentiful and the prices low. Staples are hot or cold sandwiches, such as tuna melts, ham or turkey clubs, char-grilled chicken, and pastrami. For an elegant French meal, stop into **Café 15 (50) ($$$)** *(Sofitel Lafayette Square, 806 15th St. NW, 202-730-8800, www.sofitel.com)*. Impressionistic-style paintings decorate the walls, French-pressed coffee and fresh-squeezed orange juice are guaranteed, and service is impeccable yet warm. Rub shoulders with politicians, journalists, lawyers, lobbyists, and former presidents at **The Oval**

Room (51) ($$) *(800 Connecticut Ave., 202-463-8700, www.ovalroom.com)*, featuring American cuisine with a French twist. Try **Georgia Brown's (52) ($$-$$$)** *(950 15th St. NW, 202-393-4499, www.gbrowns.com)* for southern cuisine inspired by the South Carolina low country. Catfish fingers, Carolina gumbo, or shrimp and grits are some of their specialties. Live jazz on Saturday evenings and Sunday brunch. Stop at **Caribou Coffee (53) ($)** *(17th and Pennsylvania Ave., www.cariboucoffee.com)* to relax and unwind the way the wonks do—over a newspaper or brief. For a drink other than coffee, among your best winter choices is the Apple Blast—hot cider, whipped cream, caramel, and cinnamon blended into a frothy liquid. In summer, choose a cooler—caramel, chocolate, or vanilla. For Spanish cuisine amid tapestries and lace, reserve a table at **Taberna del Alabardero (54) ($$$)** *(1776 I St. at 18th St. NW, 202-429-2200, www.alabardero.com)*. Deemed by the Spanish government the "Best Spanish Restaurant Outside of Spain," this gem offers lobster, seafood paella, and tapas—the real thing!

For **Bars & Nightlife**, try the neighboring **DOWNTOWN** area *(see page 114)*.

WHERE TO SHOP

 The museum gift shops at the **Decatur House (40)**, **Renwick Gallery (42)**, the **Corcoran Gallery of Art (43)**, and the **Daughters of the American Revolution Museum (45)** are all worth browsing for unusual, high-quality items.

WHERE TO STAY

The posh hotels here are considered pricey, but you'll love the VIP treatment. Stay at the Hay-Adams Hotel **(55) ($$$)** *(16th and H St. NW, 202-638-6600, or 800-424-5054, www.hayadams.com)* for the quintessential Washington experience—understated and elegant. Named for John Milton Hay and Henry Brooks Adams, past owners of the adjoining houses on the site, this place is reminiscent of the 1920s but somehow stays current. Ask the lobby staff to see the roof terrace used for receptions and weddings—it has a White House view not to be missed. For a grander experience, The St. Regis Washington, DC **(56) ($$$)** *(923 16th St. and K St. NW, 202-638-2626, or 888-627-8087, www.stregis.com/washington)* is the ticket. Dine in its crystal-chandeliered St. Regis Restaurant (ca. 1929) and relax in the wood-paneled Library Lounge. The spacious, Old World-style lobby is ideal for a confidential conversation. For a more contemporary environment and a different kind of DC experience, stay at the Sofitel Lafayette Square **(57) ($$-$$$)** *(806 15th St. NW, 202-730-8800, www.sofitel.com)*, DC's only 4-diamond French hotel, housed in a historic building dating from 1880. It boasts over 200 rooms and 16 suites, with exceptionally large windows. Children under 12 stay for free in their parents' room. The sleek lobby with 17-foot-high ceilings is an airy place, perfect for early morning meetings.

Washington is a city of Southern efficiency and Northern charm.

—*John F. Kennedy*

chapter 2

NATIONAL MALL

CAPITOL HILL

Places to See:

1. The Castle
2. Enid A. Haupt Garden
3. National Museum of American History
4. National Museum of Natural History
5. National Gallery of Art Sculpture Garden
6. National Gallery of Art, West Building
7. National Gallery of Art, East Building
8. National Museum of the American Indian
9. Voice of America
10. Washington Design Center
11. NATIONAL AIR AND SPACE MUSEUM ★
12. Joseph Hirshhorn Museum and Sculpture Garden
13. National Museum of African Art
14. Arthur M. Sackler Gallery
15. Freer Gallery of Art
24. U.S. CAPITOL BUILDING ★
25. U.S. Botanic Garden

26. Capitol Reflecting Pool
27. Ulysses S. Grant Memorial
28. SUPREME COURT OF THE UNITED STATES ★
29. LIBRARY OF CONGRESS ★
30. Folger Shakespeare Library
31. Sewall-Belmont House and Museum
32. Union Station
33. National Postal Museum
34. Historic Barracks Row

Places to Eat & Drink:

16. Wright Place Food Court
17. Mitsitam Café
18. Cascade Café Espresso & Gelato Bar
19. Garden Café
20. Atrium Café
21. Main Street Café
22. Smithsonian Jazz Café
35. The Monocle
36. Charlie Palmer Steak
37. Two Quail
38. B. Smith's
39. America
40. Uno Chicago Grill
41. Bistro Bis

42. Sonoma
43. Montmartre
44. White Tiger
45. Café Berlin
46. The Dubliner
47. Hawk & Dove
48. Banana Café & Piano Bar

Where to Shop:

Smithsonian Retail Stores
(located in individual museums)

Where to Stay:

All is politics in this capital.

—Thomas Jefferson

● ● *to Smithsonian, or Federal Triangle*

● ● ● ● *to L'Enfant Plaza*

● SNAPSHOT ●

The National Mall is a cornucopia of riches in the arts, science, history, and culture from throughout the world. It's not a mall as in shopping, but a grassy area extending from the Capitol to the Washington Monument, surrounded by a collection of world-class museums that can transport you to the past, the future, to foreign cultures, and back again to the United States. Whatever your passion, you will find it here. Because there is so much to do and see, familiarize yourself with the overall content, then determine your priorities so you won't be overwhelmed on your first visit, with trying to cover too much in too little time. Decide if you want your experience to be broad or deep. If you have lots of time, maybe it can be both, but most people have to choose.

The Mall is transformed into different things, depending on the season. For example, in winter, the central fountain of the National Gallery of Art Sculpture Garden turns into an ice rink. In summer, the Folklife Festival moves into full swing. And, when weather permits, the Carousel provides the young, and not so young, with a fantasyland right near the Smithsonian Castle. If you want diversity, spend a few hours or a few days at the Mall. You'll go home a different person.

PLACES TO SEE
Landmarks:

The Castle (1), formally known as the Smithsonian Institution Building *(10th St. and Independence Ave. SW, 202-633-1000)*, was designed by James Renwick, Jr. The red sandstone landmark was the Smithsonian's first building, completed in 1855. It houses the Information Center and provides a 24-minute film overview of the Smithsonian. Facing the Castle is the **Enid A. Haupt Garden (2)** *(10th St. and Independence Ave. SW)*, 4-plus acres of formal gardens and meandering pathways.

Arts & Entertainment:

The museums of the Smithsonian Institution dominate the National Mall. James Smithson (1765–1829), an English scientist who had never been to the United States, left more than $500,000 to the fledgling country to found the Smithsonian. In his lifetime, he had conducted research in chemistry, mineralogy, and geology. Since 1829, his legacy has spawned many new museums.

How and from where you approach the Mall depends on your interests. There is something for everyone, and almost all the museums have exhibits that appeal to children. Best of all, especially for families, admission is free. If you begin your Mall explorations at the west end, nearest the Washington Monument, the first building you'll notice is the **National Museum of American History (3)** *(14th St. and Constitution Ave. NW, 202-633-1000, americanhistory.si.edu)*. Four levels of exhibitions can leave you exhausted, so stop by the street-level information desk when you arrive to see what's new, what interests you, and where it is located. *(Note: The museum is closed for renovations until summer 2008.)*

If you're traveling with children, try the Hands-on Science Center, or view the ruby slippers worn by Judy Garland in *The Wizard of Oz*. Popular culture and history abound here. Be sure to see the controversial, toga-wearing 1840 sculpture of George Washington, along with first ladies' gowns. Baby boomers, take note: See Howdy Doody (the puppet) from 1950s TV. Next door is another mammoth museum, the **National Museum of Natural History (4)** *(Constitution Ave. at 10th St. NW, 202-633-1000, www.mnh.si.edu)*, housing wonders of the natural world under its dome. You can't miss the huge African elephant in the first-floor rotunda. While you're here, take in an IMAX movie, check out the 23.1-carat Carmen Lúcia ruby, or bring the kids to see the Tyrannosaurus rex and the other dinosaurs that once roamed the earth.

If it's time for a break, stop next door at the **National Gallery of Art Sculpture Garden (5)** *(9th St. and*

Constitution Ave. NW, www.nga.gov) and relax at the fountain and reflecting pool. Adjacent to the garden is the **National Gallery of Art, West Building (6)** *(6th St. and Constitution Ave. NW, 202-737-4215, www.nga.gov)*, home to major special exhibitions and a permanent collection of European and American paintings, sculpture, decorative arts, and works on paper. If time is short, pick your passion. Rembrandt's *The Mill* is in Gallery 48, Monet's *Rouen Cathedral, West Façade, Sunlight, in Gallery 85*, or da Vinci's *Ginevra de' Benci* in Gallery 6. For a more contemporary experience, head to the **National Gallery of Art, East Building (7)** *(4th St. and Constitution Ave. NW, 202-737-4215, www.nga.gov)*, designed by architect

I. M. Pei (who designed the famous Paris Louvre pyramid), and home of the renowned aluminum-and-steel, 76-foot-long Alexander Calder mobile (*Untitled*, 1976) suspended from the ceiling of the atrium. It was one of his last commissions. View the permanent modern art collections and keep your eyes open for any special exhibitions of international import.

As you cross the Mall and enter the newest addition to this area—the **National Museum of the American Indian (8)** *(4th St. and Independence Ave. SW, 202-633-1000, www.americanindian.si.edu)*—you'll hear the word "welcome" in hundreds of Native American languages. If there's time, take in the short introductory film, *Who We Are*, in the Lelawi Theater on the 4th floor. The museum showcases beadwork, pottery, textiles, paintings, and sculptures, and is the largest museum in the world devoted to American Indian art and objects. The U.S. government's international broadcasting service, **Voice of America (9)** *(330 Independence Ave. SW, 202-203-4959, www.voanews. com, tour reservations, 202-203-4990, www.voatours. com)*, broadcasts radio, television, and Internet programs in more than 50 languages to much of the world; its offices are near the Federal Center SW Metro stop. Take the family on one of its free daily tours. Browse high-end home design and home furnishing showrooms open to the public at the **Washington Design Center (10)** *(300 D St. SW, 202-646-6100, www.merchandisemart.com/dcdesigncenter)*, closest to the Federal SW Metro stop on the Orange and Blue Lines. Check out more than 70 design showrooms to see domestic and international home furnishings, fabrics, and accessories.

Continuing clockwise back toward the Mall, you'll see the ★**NATIONAL AIR AND SPACE MUSEUM (11)** *(6th St. and Independence Ave. SW, 202-633-1000, www.nasm.si.edu)*. The most-visited museum in the world, it immerses children and adults in the history of aviation and the space program. The first-floor exhibit, "Space Race," details the race to the moon between the Americans and the Soviets beginning in the early 1960s. View a variety of space suits, including one worn by U.S. astronaut John Glenn on

TOP PICK!

 his 1962 orbital flight. Another exhibit, "Milestones of Flight," chronicles aviation firsts, including the first flight of Charles Lindbergh across the Atlantic in 1927. Spend time wandering. See the Wright brothers' 1903 flyer and the Apollo 11 command module *Columbia*. Touch a lunar rock. Walk through a Skylab space station. Take the kids to the Lockheed Martin IMAX Theater to see *To Fly!*, the museum's thrilling and most popular film. You'll enjoy it, too. For an IMAX movie schedule, call 202-633-IMAX (4629). If time permits, visit the Air and Space Museum's companion exhibit hall, the **Steven F. Udvar-Hazy Center** *(14390 Air and Space Museum Parkway, Chantilly, Virginia, 202-633-2370, www.nasm. si.edu/museum/udvarhazy/)* near Washington Dulles International Airport. This mammoth facility showcases 127 aircraft and 143 large space artifacts—old, new, and experimental—including the Lockheed SR-71 Blackbird, the fastest jet in the world; the Boeing B-29 Superfortress *Enola Gay* bomber (used in the atomic mission that destroyed Hiroshima); and the first Space Shuttle, the *Enterprise*. You can also attend IMAX films here and watch air traffic at Dulles Airport from the Center's 164-foot Observation Tower.

For a complete change of atmosphere, next door to the National Air and Space Museum you'll find the **Joseph Hirshhorn Museum and Sculpture Garden (12)** *(7th St. and Independence Ave. SW, 202-633-1000, www. hirshhorn.si.edu)*. The cylindrical-shaped museum devoted to 19th- and 20th-century paintings and sculpture has an adjoining outdoor sunken garden where Miró, Moore, and Rodin sculptures abound. If you're traveling with kids, pick up a family guide packet with cards telling about different works in the permanent collection.

As you continue west, you'll find two smaller, specialized museums. The **National Museum of African Art (13)** *(950 Independence Ave. SW, 202-633-4600, www.africa.si. edu)* greets you with traditional and contemporary African music. The only American museum devoted to the collection, conservation, study, and exhibition of African art, it covers more than 900 cultures from the African continent and includes sculpture, textiles, household objects, decorative arts, and musical instruments. On the west side is the **Arthur M. Sackler Gallery (14)** *(1050 Independence Ave. SW, 202-633-4880, www.asia.si.edu)*, where you can enjoy Islamic metalwork, Japanese screens, and more. Look for *Grasping for the Moon*, an intriguing work by Chinese-born expatriate Xu Bing. The "Luxury Arts of the Silk Route Empires" exhibit is located in underground galleries connecting the **Sackler Gallery (14)** to the **Freer Gallery of Art (15)** *(Jefferson Dr. at 12th St. SW, 202-633-4880, www.asia.si.edu)*. Even if Asian art seems esoteric to you, visit the iridescent **Peacock Room** created by James McNeill Whistler for wealthy ship owner Frederick R. Leyland in 1876. The gold- and silver-painted south wall mural depicts two

fighting peacocks. The birds' brightly colored stone eyes always fascinate young children.

PLACES TO EAT & DRINK
Where to Eat:

For a quick bite or liquid refreshment while you're exploring the Mall, head for cafés within the Smithsonian Museums and the National Gallery. They're convenient and quick. Try the **Wright Place Food Court (16) ($)** *(National Air and Space Museum, 6th St. at Independence Ave. SW, 202-633-1000)* for kid-friendly selections from McDonald's, Donatos Pizza, and Boston Market. Here you will also find the **Mezza Café**, offering sandwiches, salads, and soups, plus an outdoor kiosk, weather permitting. For culinary treats with a Native American twist, the **Mitsitam**

 Café (17) ($) *(National Museum of the American Indian, 4th St. and Independence Ave. SW, 202-633-1000, www.americanindian.si.edu)* features Indian taco on frybread, smoked salmon, and buffalo burgers, as well as desserts, snacks, and beverages. For more fuel to keep your museum momentum going, stop at **Cascade Café Espresso & Gelato Bar (18) ($)** *(National Gallery of Art, East Building, 4th St. and Constitution Ave. NW, 202-737-4215, www.nga.gov).* This is a good place to relax and decide what to do next as you sample salads, soups, and wood-fired pizza. If you'd like more of a meal, head over to the **Garden Café (19) ($)** *(National Gallery of Art, West Building, 6th St.*

and Constitution Ave. NW, 202-737-4215, www.nga.gov) or the **Atrium Café (20) ($)** *(National Museum of Natural History, Constitution Ave. at 10th St. NW,*  *202-633-1000, www.mnh.si.edu).* The **Main Street Café (21) ($)** *(National Museum of American History, 14th St. and Constitution Ave. NW, 202-633-1000, www. americanhistory.si.edu; Note: Closed for renovations until summer 2008)* offers barbecue, pizza, burgers, and more; in the Palm Court, a coffee and gelato bar features espresso, pastries, and Italian ice; and Subway offers subs and salads.

Bars & Nightlife:

 On Friday evenings from Memorial Day–Labor Day, the **Smithsonian Jazz Café (22) ($)** *(National Museum of Natural History, Constitution Ave. at 10th St. NW, 202-633-1000, www.mnh.si.edu)* offers live jazz, gourmet food, drinks, and IMAX movies.

For more **Bars & Nightlife**, check out the **CAPITOL HILL** area *(see page 74).*

WHERE TO SHOP

Almost every Smithsonian museum has at least one shop, known collectively as the **Smithsonian Retail Stores** where you can shop for posters, jewelry, toys, crafts, books, and other international gift items. The museum shops are great places to find something unique and of high quality, and all are tax-free.

WHERE TO STAY

There are many hotels that are not too far from the Mall, but only one just off it: **Holiday Inn Capitol (23) ($$)** *(550 C St. SW, 202-479-4000, www.holidayinncapitol. com)*. Recently renovated and voted the number one Holiday Inn in Washington, DC by its guests, it's a convenient place to stay. It boasts a new lobby, entrance, and a hip and trendy lounge.

CAPITOL HILL

● ● *to Capitol South, or Eastern Market*

● *to Union Station*

● SNAPSHOT ●

Capitol Hill is a diverse, fascinating part of the city, where the government's legislative and judicial branches do their work. It is home to the U.S. Capitol, the U.S. Supreme Court, Library of Congress, and the House and Senate office buildings. But it is more than that. It is one of the liveliest and oldest neighborhoods in the city as well. And, with Union Station on its northern border, it is a key gateway to and from the city—intercity and high-speed trains arrive and depart every few minutes. To really enjoy this area, try not to get stuck in the government buildings unless you are a political aficionado. Consider taking the free 45-minute tour of the Capitol, but save some time to see how the rest of the world lives in the Capitol Hill Historic District. Walk the streets and take in the architectural styles. Visit the National Postal Museum. Browse Eastern Market, the city's oldest public market, dating from 1873.

PLACES TO SEE
Landmarks:

Welcome to one of the most historic and most impor-

TOP PICK!

tant structures in the United States! The ★**U.S. CAPITOL BUILDING (24)** *(Capitol Hill, east end of the National Mall, 202-225-6827, www.aoc.gov)* is the focal point of the greater Capitol Complex, including six Congressional office buildings and three Library of Congress buildings. The history of the Capitol building reflects the history of America. From the time of George Washington, it's been raised up, burnt down, reconstructed, and remodeled to adapt to a nation on the move. Today, this neoclassical structure's floor area covers more than 16 acres! Start your visit with a stroll of the building's inviting 68-acre campus; it's green and parklike, yet offers unobstructed views of the Capitol itself. This was the intent of its landscape architect, the famous Frederick Law Olmsted, who felt the grounds should be "subsidiary to the central structure." Many of the trees—especially in the eastern part of the grounds—are historic, having been planted by notable individuals and groups, or donated by various states.

A West Indies physician and amateur architect, William Thornton, won the competition to design the Capitol edifice, which resembles the Pantheon in Rome. George Washington laid the cornerstone in a Masonic ceremony in 1793; the stone has since gone missing. The initial construction of the Capitol was completed in 1800, and Congress held its first session there on November 17. In 1814, much of the interior was destroyed during the British "Burning of Washington." The Capitol was reconstructed the next year, and, several decades later, north and south wings were added. In 1866, a new fireproof cast-iron dome replaced the earlier dome made of copper-covered wood. This newer, distinctive dome is crowned by a 15,000-pound, 19-1/2-foot bronze statue of Freedom, a classical female figure symbolizing the victory of freedom in peace and war. The figure holds a U.S. shield and laurel victory wreath, wears a sword, and is capped with a helmet encircled by stars and topped with an eagle's head, feathers, and talons. Freedom was set in place in December 1863, to a 35-gun salute that was answered by the guns of 12 forts around DC. If Congress is in session, you'll notice a light below the statue. (Flags also fly over the Capitol's south House side and/or Senate north side in session.)

Inside the Capitol, the circular Rotunda, used for special state occasions, is lined with paintings and friezes of scenes from America's history; its "eye" features a mammoth fresco, *The Apotheosis of Washington*, depicting Washington rising to heaven. Painted in 1865 by Italian artist Constantino Brumidi, the work covers more than 4,600 square feet, and incorporates figures up to 15 feet tall. The Crypt space below the rotunda is used as an exhibition space. In the National Statuary Hall (The Old Hall of the House), you'll find statues of celebrated

Americans—from Samuel Adams to Brigham Young—contributed by each of the 50 states.

A brand-new subterranean **Capitol Visitor Center**, the "CVC," is slated to open in summer 2007 underneath the East Capitol grounds. This expansive facility will house orientation theaters that will show films about the House and Senate (and broadcast live feeds when Congress is in session), an exhibition gallery highlighting the Capitol's history, a 600-seat cafeteria, and gift shops.

To take the Capitol Building tour, pick up free, same-day, timed entry passes Monday–Saturday beginning at 9:00 AM at the Capitol Guide Service kiosk located at the southwest corner of the Capitol grounds at 1st Street and Independence Avenue SW. Afterward, ponder the political scene in the **Meditation Garden** at the **U.S. Botanic Garden (25)** *(1st St. and Independence Ave. SW, 202-225-8333, www.usbg.gov)*. This amazing "living museum" also features a prodigious collection of orchids and "the Jungle," a palm-filled area with a 24-foot-high viewing walkway. The new **National Garden** next door features unusual plants that grow well in the mid-Atlantic region. It also contains a butterfly garden and a rose garden. Between the Garden and the Capitol you'll

 find the **Capitol Reflecting Pool (26)** *(directly west of the Capitol)* and the **Ulysses S. Grant Memorial (27)** *(adjacent to the Capitol Reflecting Pool)*. Sculpted by Henry Shrady, it is one of the world's most intricate equestrian statues and represents the Union victory General Grant engineered during the Civil War.

East of, and within easy walking distance from the Capitol Building, you'll find the ★SUPREME COURT OF THE UNITED STATES (28) *(1st and East Capitol Sts. NE, 202-479-3030, www.supremecourtus.gov)*. You may be surprised to learn that the Court's familiar "Temple of Justice" building, its main steps flanked by the sculpted figures *Contemplation of Justice* and *Guardian of Law*, dates back only to 1935. Even though the Supreme Court was established in 1789, it had no official home, and met initially in the nation's first capital, New York City, then in Philadelphia, then in the DC Capitol. Finally, in 1929, former president and then Chief Justice William Howard Taft persuaded Congress to authorize construction of a permanent home for the Court. Popular American architect Cass Gilbert was asked to design "a building of dignity and importance." Gilbert chose a classical Corinthian style that would complement nearby congressional buildings. But Taft and Gilbert died before the building was finished, and construction was completed under Chief Justice Charles Evans Hughes and Gilbert's son, Cass Gilbert, Jr., and John R. Rockart.

At the Court's impressive west side entrance, which faces the Capitol, you'll see a pair of marble candelabra flanking the steps leading to the oval plaza in front. Carved panels on the candelabra bases depict *Justice* with sword and scales, and *The Three Fates* weaving the thread of life. Sixteen marble columns support the pediment; the words "Equal Justice Under Law" appear on the architrave above. A sculptured group over the architrave features *Liberty Enthroned*; she is guarded by *Order and Authority*. Three figures on either side of this trio, sculpted by Robert Aitken, depict the concepts of *Council and Research*. To the left, you'll see Chief Justice Taft as a youth, Secretary of State Elihu Root, and architect Cass Gilbert. On the right are Chief Justice Hughes, Aitken himself, and Chief Justice Marshall as a young man. (Few visitors see the pediment sculpture groups on the building's east side, by Hermon MacNeil. They

depict the great lawgivers Moses, Confucius, and the Greek Solon, surrounded by figures representing Means of Enforcing the Law, Tempering Justice with Mercy, and other Court concerns. The architrave says, "Justice the Guardian of Liberty.")

The Court's bronze entrance doors weigh 6-1/2 tons each. Their sculpted panels depict historic scenes in the development of law: the Shield of Achilles trial scene from the *Iliad*; a Roman praetor publishing an edict; King John sealing the Magna Carta; Lord Coke barring King James from sitting as a judge; and Chief Justice Marshall and Justice Joseph Story. Inside, double rows of marble columns line the Great Hall, and busts of former

Chief Justices are set in niches and on marble pedestals along the wall. At the east end of the Great Hall, oak doors open into the Court Chamber itself, an 82- by 91-foot room with a 44-foot ceiling, 24 columns of Siena marble, mahogany furnishings, and Beaux-Arts friezes of 18 historic lawgivers, from Egyptian king Menes, Moses, and Draco to Charlemagne, John Marshall, and Napoleon. (A sculpture of Muhammad with the Qur'an, the primary source of Islamic law, is included among the pantheon; the sculpture has been the subject of recent controversy since Islam forbids artistic depiction of religious figures. The Court's view is that the figure "is a well-intentioned attempt by the sculptor to honor Muhammad, and it bears no resemblance to Muhammad." Muslims generally have a strong aversion to sculptured or pictured representations of their Prophet.)

Beginning the first Monday in October, the Court hears two one-hour arguments a day, on Mondays, Tuesdays, and Wednesdays in two-week intervals through late April. Argument calendars are posted on the Court Web site *(www.supremecourtus.gov)* under the "Oral Arguments" link. The arguments, heard at 10:00 AM and 11:00 AM, are open to the public, but seating is limited. Before a session begins, two lines form on the plaza at the Court entrance, often hours before the building opens. One is for those wanting to hear an entire argument, the other for those wanting to observe a session briefly (3–5 minutes). Seating for the first argument begins at 9:30 AM; seating for the short-session line begins at 10:00 AM. Be ready for security screening; a coatroom and coin-operated (quarters only) lockers are available for personal belongings. Visitors are also welcome to tour the Court building, attend a free lecture, view a film, and take in exhibits about the building and the Court itself.

TOP PICK! Bibliophiles must not miss the ★**LIBRARY OF CONGRESS (29)** *(Thomas Jefferson Building, 10 1st St. at Independence Ave.; John Adams Building, 2nd St. and Independence Ave. SE; James Madison Memorial Building between 1st and 2nd Sts. and Independence Ave. SE, 202-707-8000, www.loc.gov).* This is the nation's oldest federal cultural institution, the research arm of Congress, and the largest library in the world. It contains more than 130 million items on 530 miles (!) of shelves, including 29 million books and other printed materials, 2.7 million recordings, 12 million photographs, 4.8 million maps, and 58 million manuscripts. The library occupies three buildings on Capitol Hill—its main facility, the copper-domed **Thomas Jefferson Building**, dating from 1897; the **John Adams Building**, added in 1938; and the **James Madison Memorial Building**, which opened in 1981. Established in 1800 with $5,000 appropriated by Congress, the library was housed in the new Capitol (moved from Philadelphia) until 1814, when British troops torched the building, destroying the library.

(British Prime Minister Tony Blair apologized to Congress for this in 2003.) Thomas Jefferson immediately offered his personal library of more than 6,000 books as a replacement.

Start your visit at the Library Visitors' Center, located at ground level inside the west front entrance of the Jefferson Building. The center provides interactive information kiosks and an award-winning 12-minute film in its Visitors' Theater. Docent-led tours are offered several times a day Mondays through Saturdays. The docents must complete a graduate-level training program and their tours are a great way to get acquainted with all this national treasure house has to offer. The ground floor is also home to the **Caroline and Erwin Swann Memorial Exhibit Gallery for Caricature and Cartoon**, the **George and Ira Gershwin Room**, the **Bob Hope Gallery of American Entertainment**, and the **Coolidge Auditorium**, used for chamber music concerts.

On the first floor, you'll find the library's Great Hall, with its stained-glass skylights and aluminum-leaf-finished beams. On this same floor, in the East Corridor, you'll discover two of the Library's great treasures, a Gutenberg Bible and the Giant Bible of Mainz, dating from the 1450s. On the second floor, stop by the Visitors' Gallery for great views of the domed ceiling that soars 160 feet above the Main Reading Room floor. Stained-glass representations of the seals of 48 states (excluding Alaska and Hawaii) adorn eight semicircular windows; sculptures and paintings abound. Don't miss

 the permanent-but-changing exhibition, "American Treasures of the Library of Congress." It showcases 250 rare, intriguing, or significant items, arranged like Jefferson's own library into three types of knowledge corresponding to Francis Bacon's three faculties of the mind: Memory (History), Reason (Philosophy), and Imagination (Fine Arts).

Stroll the exterior of the Jefferson Building. King Neptune and his court cavort in the famous fountain out front. The first-story window keystones are accented by a series of ethnological heads (33 in all), from Arab to Zulu; they're based on a Smithsonian Institution collection. On the second-story level, busts of nine great men grace the front entrance pavilion: Demosthenes, Emerson, Irving, Goethe, Franklin, Macaulay, Hawthorne, Scott, and Dante.

Those 18 and over can obtain a Library of Congress user card. Bring a driver's license or passport to the Madison Building's Reader Registration Room, LM 140 *(ground floor)*. All materials must be used on-site.

Arts & Entertainment:

Next to the **Library of Congress (29)** Adams building is the **Folger Shakespeare Library (30)** *(201 E. Capitol St. SE, 202-544-4600, www.folger.edu, open Monday through Saturday)*, the gift of oil executive Henry Clay Folger. This library holds the first published edition of Shakespeare's comedies, histories, and tragedies, printed in 1623, along with thousands of other books, manuscripts, and items related to the Bard and his work. Inside the building is a reproduction of a 16th-century theater, which stages performances of chamber music, baroque opera, and Shakespearean plays.

Walking east and north of the Capitol Building lies the 19th-century Capitol Hill Historic District, known as Jenkins Hill. During the early years of the Republic, few members of Congress established permanent residences in the city. Instead, they chose to live in boardinghouses from which they could walk to the Capitol. Today, the neighborhood is a collection of row houses from later architectural periods, including Federal, Italianate, Second Empire, Romanesque, Queen Anne, and Classical Revival. It's a feast for the eyes. One of them, the **Sewall-Belmont House and Museum (31)** *(144 Constitution Ave. NE 1st/2nd Sts., 202-546-1210, www.sewallbelmont.org)*, was for 43 years the home of Alice Paul, National Woman's Party founder and author of the Equal Rights Amendment. Today, it is a museum dedicated to the early women's rights movement. From there, walk north on First Street to **Union Station (32)** *(50 Massachusetts Ave. NE at 1st St., www.unionstationdc. com)*. Unlike most railroad stations you've seen, this one is a 1908 Beaux-Arts building restored to the height of its beauty. It's a world unto itself, with a state-of-the-art 9-screen movie complex, an international food court, and two levels of trendy specialty shops. It's more than a transportation hub: imagine a Presidential Inaugural Ball here under the 96-foot, gilded waiting room ceiling and you'll get the picture. Just west of the station is the **National Postal Museum (33)** *(2 Massachusetts Ave. at 1st St. NE, 202-633-1000, www.postalmuseum.si.edu).*

Whether you are a stamp collector or not, it's worth a visit. From the vintage airmail planes hanging from the 90-foot-high atrium to stagecoaches, rare stamps, and interactive exhibits (one of which allows you to create postcards to send home), it's a fun, free philatelic experience for the family. **Historic Barracks Row (34)** *(south of Eastern Market Metro Plaza, on 8th St., 202-544-3188, www.barracksrow.org)* is the oldest post of the U.S. Marine Corps, and the place where composer John Philip Sousa worked from 1880–1892. If you're here

on a Friday evening in summer, you might catch the weekly evening parade and free band performance (reservations are generally required, however). Recently revitalized, the area is enlivened by charming shops and restaurants.

PLACES TO EAT & DRINK
Where to Eat:

Eateries of all varieties abound in this area. From family favorites to power lunches, and from the posh to the trendy, you'll find a plethora of dining options. For an established (1960) seafood and meat restaurant where deals are sealed near the Senate side of the Capitol, **The Monocle (35) ($$-$$$)** *(107 D St. NE, 202-546-4488, www.themonocle.com)* is as reliable as it gets. If you prefer a sleek steak and seafood choice with American wine and a view of the Capitol, try **Charlie Palmer Steak (36) ($$-$$$)** *(101 Constitution Ave. NW, 202-547-8100, www.charliepalmer.com)*. For a great romantic spot, Washington insiders book a table in one of the cozy dining nooks at **Two Quail (37) ($$-$$$)** *(320 Massachusetts Ave. NE, 202-543-8030, www.twoquail.com)*. Wing chairs and mismatched china add to the charm. Try the signature dish, two quail stuffed with pumpkin and apple filling, topped with a Jack Daniel's cider sauce. Other choices include filet mignon, broiled scallops, and seafood penne pasta. Top off the evening with a carriage ride through Capitol Hill. For many food choices in one place, **Union Station (32)** offers cafés, casual dining, and restaurants. One of the most distinctive is **B. Smith's (38) ($$-$$$)** *(50 Massachusetts Ave. NE, 202-289-6188, www.bsmith.com)*, offering Cajun, Creole, and Southern cuisine in "one of the most beautiful dining rooms in America." **America (39) ($)** *(50 Massachusetts Ave. NE, 202-682-9555, www.ark restaurants.com)*, also tempts tastebuds with more than 200 traditional dishes in the Main Hall, street level. **Uno Chicago Grill (40) ($)** *(50 Massachusetts Ave. NE, 202-842-0438, www.unos.com)*

serves Chicago-style pizza and other casual crowd-pleasers perfect for families. You'll find it on the mezzanine level. **Bistro Bis (41) ($$)** *(15 E St. NW, 202-661-2700, www.bistrobis.com)* in the Hotel George (52) features French food and wine in a modern setting where you're likely to spot senators and house members. For wood-grilled meats, handmade pasta, and pizza, visit **Sonoma (42) ($-$$)** *(223 Pennsylvania Ave. SE, 202-544-8088, www.sonomadc.com)*. If you're adventurous, head over to 8th Street SE, where a new restaurant row is burgeoning. **Montmartre (43) ($$)** *(327 7th St. SE, 202-544-1244, www.montmartre.us)* transports you to Paris with authentic French favorites and alfresco seating. For a taste of the light, northern Indian fare that draws the Capitol Hill crowd, track down the **White Tiger (44) ($)** *(301 Massachusetts Ave. NE, 202-546-5900, www.WhiteTigerDC.com)*. Turkey kabob, spiced calamari, samosas, soups, and salads dot the menu. Treat yourself Teutonic style at **Café Berlin (45) ($$)** *(322 Massachusetts Ave. NE, 202-543-7656, www.cafeberlindc.com)*, where schnitzel, marinated herring, traditional desserts like Black Forest cake, and German beers and wines draw politicians and locals.

Bars & Nightlife:

Mix and mingle at **The Dubliner (46)** *(520 N. Capitol St. NW, 202-638-6900, phoenixparkhotel.com)*, offering pub favorites like fish and chips and shepherd's pie while you enjoy live Irish music, and beers and ales, including

Old Dubliner Amber Ale. A typical Capitol Hill watering hole, **Hawk & Dove (47)** *(329 Pennsylvania Ave. SE, 202-543-3300, www.hawkanddoveonline.com)* is a vibrant gathering place for both Democrats and Republicans. The bar's six rooms allow for a large gathering or an intimate conversation in front of the fireplace. For a colorful experience, visit the **Banana Café & Piano Bar (48)** *(500 8th St. SE, 202-543-5906, www.bananacafedc. com)* for Cuban, Puerto Rican, and Mexican dishes, and live piano music on the second floor. It's a fun place decorated in vibrant lime green, tangerine, and pink accented with local art.

WHERE TO SHOP

Have fun browsing at Eastern Market (49) *(225 7th and C Sts. SE, 202-544-0083, www.easternmarketdc.com, closed Mondays)*, where shopping is a daily art. Housed in a 19th-century brick building designed by Adolf Cluss, the market is the centerpiece of this old-fashioned neighborhood. Try the South Hall, a public market, for fresh produce, flowers, bakery items, poultry, and cheese. The North Hall is an arts and community center. On weekends, there's a flea market filled with antiques and crafts. Farmers also bring their wares from Maryland, Virginia, Pennsylvania, and West Virginia—some from families who have been coming since the market was built. Pulp on the Hill (50) *(303 Pennsylvania Ave. SE at 3rd St., 202-543-1924, www.pulpdc.com)* offers offbeat cards, paper goods, and gifts. You'll also find the work of local and established artists here.

Otherwise, a trip to East Hall (51) at **Union Station (32)** *(50 Massachusetts Ave. NE, 202-289-1908, www.unionstationdc.com)* will yield great gift items, such as jewelry, scarves, decorative boxes, and novelties. You'll browse your way through a visual journey around the world.

WHERE TO STAY

If you like being in the center of activity, this area is for you. Most hotels are clustered between Capitol Hill and **Union Station (32)** to the north, near the Senate side. If you prefer contemporary to conventional, stay at the hip Hotel George (52) ($$-$$$) *(15 E St. NW, 202-347-4200 or 800-576-8331, www. hotelgeorge.com)*, a boutique hotel with stylish, sleek yet comfortable rooms. For traditional on a grand scale, choose the Hyatt Regency on Capitol Hill (53) ($$-$$$) *(400 New Jersey Ave. NW, 202-737-1234, www.hyattregencywashington.com)*, with its five-story atrium. At the Phoenix Park Hotel (54) ($$-$$$) *(520 N. Capitol St. NW, 202-638-6900, phoenixparkhotel.com)*,

Celtic charm abounds. For a different atmosphere on the House side, Capitol Hill Suites (55) ($-$$) *(200 C St. SE, 202-543-6000, www.capitolhillsuites.com)*, located on a quiet residential street, offers 152 rooms; its patrons include

6000, www.capitolhillsuites.com), located on a quiet residential street, offers 152 rooms; its patrons include those working at the Library of Congress. Rates are better on the weekends when life on the Hill slows down. Family-friendly **Holiday Inn on the Hill (56) ($$)** *(415 New Jersey Ave. NW, 202-638-1616 or 800-638-1116, www.hionthehilldc.com)* is newly renovated with a rooftop pool and sundeck. The **Washington Court Hotel on Capitol Hill (57) ($$$)** *(525 New Jersey Ave. NW, 202-628-2100 or 800-321-3010, www. washingtoncourthotel.com)* is a boutique-style hotel, known for its exceptional service.

chapter 3

GEORGETOWN AND WASHINGTON HARBOUR

FOGGY BOTTOM

GEORGETOWN AND WASHINGTON HARBOUR FOGGY BOTTOM

Places to See:

1. Old Stone House
2. Chesapeake and Ohio (C&O) Canal
3. Washington Harbour
4. Tudor Place Historic House and Garden
5. Dumbarton Oaks and Gardens
6. Dumbarton House
7. 3260 N Street
8. 3307 N Street
9. 3038 N Street
10. Georgetown University
11. Francis Scott Key Memorial Park
59. Federal Reserve Board Building
60. National Academy of Sciences
61. Albert Einstein Memorial
62. U.S. Department of State Diplomatic Reception Rooms
63. George Washington University
64. Lisner Auditorium
65. International Monetary Fund Center
66. World Bank
67. U.S. Department of Interior Museum
68. John F. Kennedy Center for the Performing Arts
69. Thompson Boat Center
70. B'nai B'rith Klutznick National Jewish Museum Collection and Gallery
71. Arts Club of Washington

Places to Eat & Drink:

12. La Chaumière
13. 1789 Restaurant
14. Neyla
15. Filomena Ristorante
16. Café Milano
17. Morton's of Chicago
18. Peacock Café
19. Bangkok Bistro
20. Café Bonaparte
21. Café La Ruche
22. Clyde's of Georgetown
23. Michel Richard Citronelle
24. Seasons

Where to Stay:

Where to Shop:

GEORGETOWN AND
WASHINGTON HARBOUR

●● *to Foggy Bottom/GWU*

● SNAPSHOT ●

Georgetown is one of the liveliest and most historic neighborhoods in the Washington, DC, area. It retains its cachet as the separate town it once was in 1751, when it was named in honor of King George II. Because of its desirability as a port, the U.S. Congress decided to annex it to the city of Washington in 1871. Situated on the Potomac River, Georgetown developed as a commercial and industrial hub around Washington Harbour, prospering from shipping and tobacco. Through the years, prosperity has ebbed and flowed, but Georgetown kept its reputation, and, so far, has managed to keep the Metro out of the neighborhood. It is connected by numerous Metro buses to the closest Metro stop, Foggy Bottom, and by the DC Circulator bus (*see page 8*) to Union Station and the Washington Convention Center. What makes Georgetown great is its location on the Potomac, and its distinctive charm and character, from its tree-lined streets and plentiful restaurants, taverns, shops, and hotels, to its renowned residents and historic architecture, including Georgian, Federal, and Classical Revival styles.

PLACES TO SEE
Landmarks:

M Street running east to west, and Wisconsin Avenue, running northwest to south, are the main thoroughfares in Georgetown. Some major landmarks date back to the mid-1700s, transporting you to another era. The **Old Stone House (1)** *(3051 M St. NW, 202-426-6851, www.nps.gov/rocr/olst)* is a reminder of Georgetown's 18th-century past. Dating to 1765, it's one of the oldest structures in Washington, DC, and a superb example of colonial life in America. Another way to experience Georgetown's past as you soak up some of today's atmosphere is to stroll the towpath once used by mules or ride a canal barge along the **Chesapeake and Ohio (C&O) Canal (2)** *(National Park Service Visitor's Center, 1057 Thomas Jefferson St. NW, just south of M St., 202-653-5190, www.nps.gov/choh)*. Period-costumed guides lead the hour-long barge ride, a great way to relax and learn. After walking south to the bottom of Thomas Jefferson Street, catch the view of **Washington Harbour (3)** *(3000 K St. NW)* from the boardwalk, where

the central fountain court sends sprays of water up against the backdrop of the Potomac. Visit at sunset or twilight for a romantic rendezvous. Head north of M Street, the main thoroughfare, and follow 31st Street north. The real Georgetown lies off the major arteries, where Federal-era mansions and town houses abound, including those made famous by President John F. Kennedy and his family. These are now private residences. **Tudor Place Historic House and Garden (4)** *(1644 31st St. NW, 202-965-0400, www.tudorplace.org)*, once the home of Martha Washington's granddaughter, Martha Custis Peter, is a lovely example of Federal architecture and features a domed roof portico. Peter, who purchased the land with a legacy from her grandmother, planted some of the property's boxwoods in the five-acre garden herself. A few minutes further north, you'll find **Dumbarton Oaks and Gardens (5)** *(1703 32nd St. NW, 202-339-6401, www.doaks.org)*, a 10-acre garden of formal terraces, garden rooms, and naturalistic areas; Dumbarton Oaks, an 1801 Federal mansion owned by Harvard University, maintains collections of Byzantine and Pre-Columbian art and rare books. A few blocks southeast is the **Dumbarton House (6)** *(2715 Q St., 27th/28th Sts. NW, 202-337-2288, www.dumbartonhouse.org)*, another Federal house. If period furniture and decorative arts of the late 18th- and early 19th-centuries are your fancy, take a docent-led tour. If you're a Kennedy family buff, wander south to N Street to see some of their family homes. JFK lived in **3260 N Street (7)** when he began his Senate career. He purchased **3307 N Street (8)** for Jackie after the birth of their daughter Caroline in 1957. Jackie, Caroline, and John Jr. lived in **3038 N Street (9)** temporarily after JFK's assassination. Georgetown is also the home of **Georgetown University (10)** *(37th and O Sts. NW, 202-687-0100, www.georgetown.edu)*, the oldest Catholic university in the U.S. The tower of its Healy Hall, a Romanesque Revival structure, features prominently in the city's skyline. For a bit of green, find solace at the **Francis Scott Key Memorial Park (11)** *(M St. 34th St./Key Bridge)*.

PLACES TO EAT & DRINK
Where to Eat:

Georgetown has more restaurants than almost any Washington, DC, neighborhood. One of its best dining spots for food, ambience, and service is **La Chaumière (12) ($$)** *(2813 M St. NW, 202-338-1784, www.lachaumieredc.com)*, an award-winning French country "inn" that draws a crowd even on weekday nights. Leave room for the chocolate or Grand Marnier soufflé, a house specialty. A good choice for formal occasions is **1789 Restaurant (13) ($$$)** *(1226 36th St. at Prospect St., 202-965-1789, www.1789 restaurant.com)* located in a renovated Federal house near the university. Try its signature rack of lamb or crab cakes. For Mediterranean cuisine in an exotic atmosphere—with pillows, dim lighting, and international music—choose **Neyla (14) ($$)** *(3206 N St. NW, 202-333-6353, www.neyla.com)*. Celebrities, politicos, and tourists alike gather at **Filomena Ristorante (15) ($$-$$$)** *(1063 Wisconsin Ave. NW, 202-338-8800, www.filomena.com)* to watch the "mamas" make homemade pasta. For trendier venues, four places on Prospect Street, one block north of M Street and one block west of Wisconsin, are magnets. **Café Milano (16) ($$$)** *(3251 Prospect St. NW, 202-333-6183, www.cafemilano.net)* offers new Italian food and a high level of service. **Morton's of Chicago (17) ($$$)** *(3251 Prospect St., NW, 202-342-6258, www.mortons.com)* serves steak in a "power" atmosphere. **Peacock Café (18) ($$)** *(3251 Prospect St. NW, 202-625-2740, www.peacockcafe.com)* provides an eclectic, contemporary American menu. For Asian and Thai food in a casual setting, try **Bangkok Bistro (19) ($)** *(3251 Prospect St. NW, 202-337-2424)*. Further up Wisconsin Avenue, there's a treat not to be missed: **Café Bonaparte (20) ($-$$)** *(1522 Wisconsin Ave. NW, P St./ Volta Pl., 202-333-8830, www.cafe bonaparte.com)*, a tiny European-style crêperie, coffee shop, and bistro bar, is

as good as it is authentic. For delectable pastries, **Café La Ruche (21) ($)** *(1039 31st St. NW, 202-965-2684, www.cafelaruche.com)*, which bills itself as "a bit of Paris on the Potomac," is a Georgetown institution south of M Street. Another reliable place for great burgers and other informal fare is **Clyde's of Georgetown (22) ($)** *(3236 M St. NW, 202-333-9180, www.clydes.com)*, the unique local chain's original location. The hit song "Afternoon Delight" was inspired by its late-afternoon appetizer menu; the gold record hangs in the restaurant. For a special evening out featuring the very best California/French cuisine, **Michel Richard Citronelle (23) ($$$)** *(3000 M St. NW, 202-625-2150, www.citronelledc.com)* is the ticket. Internationally acclaimed chef Michel Richard offers inventive twists on lamb, rabbit, lobster, and venison. A main dining room "mood wall" constantly changes color. **Seasons (24) ($$$)** *(2800 Pennsylvania Ave. 202-342-0444, www. fourseasons.com)* at the Four Seasons Hotel (53) also offers exceptional cuisine and service. Another top spot is **Fahrenheit (25) ($$$)** *(Ritz-Carlton, 3100 South St. NW, 202-912-4110, www.ritzcarlton.com)*, where sleek, industrial decor sets the stage for a special evening. For meat loaf, mashed potatoes, and fresh-baked fruit cobbler, count on **Daily Grill (26) ($$)** *(1310 Wisconsin Ave. NW, 202-337-4900)*. If you prefer fish, try the filet of sole entrée or the salmon with ginger appetizer. For Mediterranean, **Cilantro Restaurant & Tapas Bar (27) ($$)** *(3241 M St. NW, 202-625-6247, www.cilantrobistro.com)* tempts you with hot and cold tapas and *mezze*, from coco shrimp to baba ganoush. There are grilled kebabs, pasta, and risotto, too. And don't forget the heavenly pizza at **Pizzeria Paradiso (28) ($)** *(3282 M St. NW, 202-337-1245, www. eatyourpizza.com)*. Mix with Georgetown students at **The Tombs (29) ($)** *(1226 36th St. NW, 202-337-6668)*, where homemade soup is a bargain. For fresh seafood and fantastic Potomac views, head to the Washington Harbour at dusk and **Tony & Joe's Seafood Place (30) ($$)** *(3000 K St. NW, 202-944-4545, www.dcseafood.com)*.

Bars & Nightlife:

Trendy **Sequoia (31)** *(3000 K St. NW, 202-944-4200, www.arkrestaurants.com)* has an enormous bar on the ground floor with outdoor tables; it also boasts great views and a varied American menu. Georgetown's famous **Blues Alley (32)** *(1073 Wisconsin Ave. NW, south of M St., 202-337-4141, www.bluesalley.com)* is a first-rate jazz and supper club where artists like Tony Bennett, Wynton Marsalis, and Nancy Wilson perform. Relax with Washington's power elite at the **Degrees Bar & Lounge (33)** *(Ritz-Carlton, 3100 South St. NW, 202-912-4100, www.ritzcarlton.com)*, in the Ritz-Carlton (57). The lounge exudes 1940s style. Try the "Fahrenheit Five" martini, the hotel's specialty. For sophisticated cocktails, low-key conversation, and an over-25 crowd, try the upper level of stylish **Blue Gin (34)** *(1206 Wisconsin Ave. NW, 202-965-5555, www.bluegindc.com)*. **Martin's Tavern (35)** *(1264 Wisconsin Ave., north of M St., 202-333-7370, www.martins-tavern.com)* has been around since 1933, attracting every president from Harry Truman to "W," as well as locals and tourists, to its famous mahogany bar.

WHERE TO SHOP

Georgetown is an eclectic mix of home furnishing stores, clothing boutiques, gift shops, and ice cream and sweets emporiums. Unique gift items are abundant. For handcrafted design, check out Appalachian Spring (36) *(1415 Wisconsin Ave. NW, 202-337-5780)* for quilts, blown glass, wood sculptures, colorful pottery, and jewelry. Atrium Interiors (37) *(1425 Wisconsin Ave. NW, 202-333-0763, www.atrium-interiors.com)* offers European-style, custom-made, solid wood furniture. For fine crystal, china, and linens, Baldaquin (38) *(1413 Wisconsin Ave. NW, 202-625-1600, www.baldaquin.com)* excels with top names. Further up the hill, north of M Street, Space Fine Furniture (39) (1625 Wisconsin Ave. NW, 202-333-0140) carries 19th- and mid-20th-century pieces reupholstered in modern fabrics. Imagine a 1940s wing chair done in shiny patent leather; you'll find it here. A Mano, Ltd. (40) (1677 Wisconsin Ave. NW, 202-298-7200, www.amanoinc.com)—"a mano" means "by hand"—carries French and Italian hand-painted tableware, crystal, china, and linens. Sassanova (41) (1641 Wisconsin Ave. NW, 202-471-4400, www.sassanova.com)

 stocks high-end shoes, handbags, and jewelry. The Phoenix (42) (1514 Wisconsin Ave. NW, 202-338-4404) has been selling contemporary clothes and handcrafted gift items since 1955. For a one-stop shop for designer clothing, shoes, and sunglasses from Marc Jacobs, Moschino, and Versace, Focus (43) (1330 Wisconsin Ave. NW, 202-337-8969) is your best bet. Proper Topper (44) (3213 P St. NW, 202-333-6200, www.propertopper.com) will win you over with its whimsical hats, jewelry, purses, accessories, games, and menswear. Check out the **Shops at Georgetown Park**, such as Intermix (45) (3222 M St. NW, 202-298-5577, www.intermixonline.com), a Madison Avenue-based retailer of trendy women's wear. Wander the Victorian-style four-story mall for other name-brand shops. Stitch DC (46) (1071 Wisconsin Ave. NW, 202-333-KNIT, www.stitchdc.com) carries yarn in every color of the rainbow. Stop at Leonidas Chocolates (47) (1531 Wisconsin Ave. NW, 202-944-1898, www.leonidasdc.com) for

Belgian chocolates and confectionaries. Dean & Deluca (48) *(3276 M St. NW, 202-342-2500, www.deandeluca. com)* is as good as it gets for gourmet fare. If you're looking for antiques and paintings, browse the shops near the Four Seasons Hotel (53), such as Gallery Lareuse (49) *(2820 Pennsylvania Ave. NW, 202-333-1506)*, showcasing works by Europeans and Americans, or Justine Mehlman Antiques (50) *(2824 Pennsylvania Ave. NW, 202-337-0419)* for Art Nouveau, arts & crafts, and Art Deco designs. For Lalique, Gallé, Tiffany, and Steuben, stop by Cherub Antiques Gallery (51) *(2918 M St. NW, 202-337-2224)*. Take a trip down memory lane at Animation Sensations (52) *(2909-1/2 M St. NW, 202-338-1097, www.animationsensations.com)*, where Disney and Warner Brothers animation art cels, drawings, and production backgrounds are available to buy or browse.

WHERE TO STAY

Be pampered at the Four Seasons Hotel (53) ($$$) *(2800 Pennsylvania Ave. NW, 202-342-0444, www.fourseasons. com)* on the eastern edge of Georgetown. For an upscale "see-and-be-seen" experience, stop by its lobby lounge for cocktails and hors d'oeuvres. Diplomats and film stars choose The Georgetown Inn (54) ($$-$$$) *(1310 Wisconsin Ave. NW, 202-333-8900 or 1-800-368-5922, www.georgetowninn.com)*. It exudes Old-World elegance, and is famed for its anticipate-your-every-need service. For quaint European style, stay at the Inn's sister property, The Latham Hotel (55) ($$-$$$) *(3000 M St. NW, 202-726-5000 or 1-800-368-5922, www.thelatham.com)*, overlooking the C&O Canal. For all the comforts of home, stay at Georgetown Suites (56) ($$-$$$) *(1111 30th St. NW and 1000 29th St. NW, 202-298-7800 or 800-348-7203, www.georgetownsuites.com)*; fully equipped kitchens and complimentary breakfast are included. The newest property in Georgetown, the intriguing Ritz-Carlton (57) ($$$) *(3100 South St. NW, 202-912-4100 or 1-800-241-3333, www.ritzcarlton.com)* is located in a historic 1932 incinerator building with smokestack. Don't miss its lobby lounge—the fireplace crackles in winter, warming the red brick interior that's accented with leather ottomans and upholstered chairs and sofas. For reasonable rates, book the Holiday Inn Georgetown (58) ($-$$) *(2101 Wisconsin Ave. NW, 202-338-4600, www.higeorgetown.com)*. This recently renovated hotel offers traditional accommodations and dining.

● ● *to Foggy Bottom/GWU, or Farragut West*

● SNAPSHOT ●

Foggy Bottom, also known as the West End, is a stately neighborhood between Georgetown and Lafayette Square. It's home to the U.S. Department of State, part of the National Academy of Sciences, the International Monetary Fund, Watergate, the Federal Reserve, the John F. Kennedy Center for the Performing Arts, George Washington University, and some of the best restaurants in the Capital City. The residential neighborhood near the Foggy Bottom Metro stop is lined with charming 19th-century town houses, former homes of the area's earliest residents: working-class Irish, Germans, and African Americans. Smoke from the factories in which they worked produced continual fog along the Potomac waterfront here, hence the name "Foggy Bottom." Today, expensive condominiums have sprung up in the neighborhood, and a number of high-end hotels dot the area. The distance to points of interest can be a bit far from the Foggy Bottom Metro stop. You might want to rely on buses from Georgetown or Lafayette Square instead, as several key places are clustered together along Constitution Avenue and west of 18th Street.

PLACES TO SEE
Landmarks:

Start by walking west on Constitution to the **Federal Reserve Board Building (59)** *(Constitution Ave. NW, 20th/21st Sts., 202-452-3324, www.federalreserve.gov)*, a commanding marble building that houses the watchdogs of the U.S. economy. Pre-arranged group tours are offered and require 24-hours advance notice. To view the changing art exhibits, call 202-452-3778. Next door is the **National Academy of Sciences (NAS) (60)** *(2101 Constitution Ave. NW, 202-334-2436, www.nationalacademies.org/arts)*, the organization that advises the U.S. Congress of breakthroughs and studies in medicine, science, and engineering. Free concerts by internationally renowned musicians take place in the auditorium on Sunday afternoons. Enter at 2100 C Street NW. In the southwest corner of the Academy

grounds, you'll find the **Albert Einstein Memorial (61)** *(2101 Constitution Ave. NW)*. The 12-foot bronze statue portrays the scientist seated, holding a sheet of mathematical equations. A 28-foot celestial map is at his feet. One block north on C Street, the **U.S. Department of State Diplomatic Reception Rooms (62)** *(2201 C St. NW, 202-647-3241, http://receptiontours.state.gov)* houses a superb collection of 18th-century American paintings, furniture, and decorative arts, including pieces by Revere and Chippendale. Reservations are required 90 days in advance for this fine arts tour.

George Washington University (63) (*F St. NW, 19th/23rd Sts., www.gwu.edu*) was founded in 1822; its campus is filled with Colonial Revival architecture. Also located on campus is **Lisner Auditorium (64)** (*730 21st St. NW, 202-994-1500, www.lisner.org*). The public is invited to its music, dance, and theater programs. Nearby is the **International Monetary Fund Center (65)** (*720 19th St. NW, 202-623-6869, www.imf.org/center*), where you can view the permanent exhibit, "Money Matters." You can also tour the nearby **World Bank (66)** (*1818 H St. NW, 202-473-1000, www.worldbank.com*), which provides financial and technical assistance to developing countries throughout the world. To learn more visit the adjacent **J Building InfoShop** (*701 18th St. NW, 202-458-4500*).

Arts & Entertainment:

If wildlife, Native American affairs, land management, and geology interest you, you might enjoy the dioramas and murals of the **U.S. Department of Interior Museum (67)** (*1849 C St. NW, 202-208-4743, www.doi.gov/museum*). Though this neighborhood is dominated by university and federal buildings, it also boasts a top arts venue, the **John F. Kennedy Center for the Performing Arts (68)** (*2700 F St. NW, 202-467-4600, www.kennedy-center.org*), where you can enjoy a concert, play, opera, or dance performance. A free **Kennedy Center Show Shuttle** runs back and forth between the Center and the Foggy Bottom Metro stop. Free daily performances take place at the **Millennium Stage**. Many of the Kennedy Center furnishings were donated by other

countries, including the impressive Orrefors crystal chandeliers from Sweden in the foyer and the white Carrara marble from Italy. Stroll the landscaped terrace overlooking the Potomac before or after. For outdoor diversion, **Thompson Boat Center (69)** *(2900 Virginia Ave. NW, 202-333-9543, www.thompsonboatcenter.com)* rents canoes, rowing shells, and kayaks, and offers group lessons as well. If you're a landlubber, choose an all-terrain bike instead.

To learn about the history and contributions of the Jewish people, visit the **B'nai B'rith Klutznick National Jewish Museum Collection and Gallery (70)** *(2020 K St. NW, 202-857-6583, www.bnaibrith.org/museum, by advance reservation only)*. It's the home of George Washington's 1790 letter to the Touro Synagogue in Rhode Island, pledging "to bigotry no sanction." Another cultural venue is the **Arts Club of Washington (71)** *(2017 I St. NW, 202-331-7282, www.artsclubof washington.org)*, the oldest nonprofit arts organization in the city. It offers free concerts, seminars, and literary events in an 1805 Georgian-style house, once the home of President James Monroe. Its galleries are open to the public free of charge Tuesdays–Saturdays.

PLACES TO EAT & DRINK
Where to Eat:
It's exciting to be able to choose from so many top-notch restaurants in one place. But they're all popular;

be sure to plan ahead and reserve early if there's a special place you want to experience while you're here. Among the best is **Marcel's (72) ($$$)** *(2401 Pennsylvania Ave. NW, 202-296-1166, www.marcelsdc. com)*, serving French cuisine with a Flemish accent. A pre-theater menu includes complimentary limo service to and from the Kennedy Center. Return afterward for dessert and jazz piano in the wine bar. Another DC favorite is **Kinkead's (73) ($$-$$$)** *(2000 Pennsylvania Ave. NW, 202-296-7700, www.kinkead.com)*, where the food is tops and the atmosphere convivial. Try the pepita-crusted salmon or fried clams. For cheap eats, there's **Au Bon Pain (74) ($)** *(2000 Pennsylvania Ave. NW, 202-887-9215)*. At **Aquarelle (75) ($$-$$$)** *(2650 Virginia Ave. NW, 202-298-4455, www. thewatergatehotel.com)* in the famed Watergate Hotel, you (and celebrities) dine overlooking the Potomac River. The cuisine is Mediterranean and Pacific Rim-inspired, with scallops and foie gras featured. For a pre-concert or pre-theater meal, **DISH (76) ($$)** *(924 25th St. NW, I/K Sts., 202-338-8707, www.dishdc.com)* at the River Inn offers warm ambience, complete with a fireplace and American classics. **Roof Terrace Restaurant and Bar (77) ($$-$$$)** *(2700 F St. NW, 202-416-8555, www.kennedy-center.org, shuttle from Foggy Bottom Metro stop every 15 min.)* offers an unforgettable dining experience that includes modern American food and a panoramic view of the Potomac. **The Colonnade (78) ($$$)** *(2401 M St. NW, 202-457-5000, www. fairmont.com)* is renowned for its sumptuous Sunday brunch with free-flowing Taittinger champagne.

600 Restaurant at the Watergate (79) ($$-$$$) *(Watergate complex, 600 New Hampshire Ave. NW, 202-337-5890, www.600restaurant.com)* draws high-level State Department officials, senators, and everyone who appreciates fine cuisine. Allow at least two hours for your meal. Try the sea bass, Australian rack of lamb, vegetarian pasta, or three-course prix fixe dinner. For upscale Asian, book a table at **Asia Nora (80) ($$-$$$)** *(2213 M St. NW, 202-797-4860, www.noras.com)*.

Bars & Nightlife:

If you enjoy sipping wine while listening to live piano music, stop at **The Wine Bar (72)** *(Marcel's, 2401 Pennsylvania Ave. NW, 202-296-1166)*. The **Library Bar (81)** *(Melrose Hotel, 2430 Pennsylvania Ave. NW 202-955-6400, www.melrosehoteldc.com)* is where the "in-the-know" Washingtonians come to see and be seen. If you don't want to miss viewing your favorite New York sports teams, watch them at **The 51st State Tavern (82)** *(2512 L St. NW, 202-635-2444, www.51ststatetavern.com)*; it boasts several TV screens, including a 60-inch plasma TV, as well as antique bars on two floors, Internet jukeboxes, and a pool table.

WHERE TO SHOP

This area is not known for its shopping, as Georgetown is, but there are some real finds at the small upscale stores located in the Watergate Shops (83) *(2522 Virginia Ave. NW)*. For example, within this six-building complex you'll find a **Saks Jandel Boutique**, which carries Valentino, Louis Feraud, Yves St. Laurent, and a Vera

Wang bridal shop. The Indian Craft Shop (84) *(1849 C St. NW, 202-208-4056)*, located within the U.S. Department of Interior Museum (67), sells authentic Native American jewelry, pottery, and handwoven rugs.

WHERE TO STAY

For luxury, elegance, and a newly renovated state-of-the-art health club, The Fairmont Washington, DC (85) ($$-$$$) *(2401 M St. NW, 202-429-2400 or 800-441-1414, www.fairmont.com/washington)* is a great choice. The Park Hyatt Washington (86) ($$$) *(24th and M Sts. NW, 202-789-1234 or 800-778-7477, www.parkhyatt washington.com)*, with a $24 million redesign completed in 2006, captures modern style with contemporary lighting, wooden blinds, and authentic folk art. The Melrose Hotel (87) ($$-$$$) *(2430 Pennsylvania Ave. NW, 202-955-6400 or 800-MELROSE, www.melrosehoteldc. com)* has rooms and suites that are among the largest in the city, as well as total Wi-Fi and high-speed Internet. A plush boutique hotel, The River Inn (88) ($$-$$$) *(924 25th St. NW, 202-337-7600 or 800-424-2741, www. theriverinn.com)* offers cozy comfort. The West End Ritz-Carlton, Washington, DC (89) ($$$) *(1150 22nd St. on M St. NW, 202-835-0500 or 800-241-3333, www. ritzcarlton.com)* has it all—goose-down pillows, marble tubs, spa, and afternoon tea. For spectacular views of the Potomac and easy access to the Kennedy Center, stay at the Watergate Hotel (90) ($$$) *(2650 Virginia Ave. NW, 202-965-2300, www.thewatergatehotel.com)* of the infamous presidential scandal. The hotel ranks high for its luxury suites.

chapter 4

DOWNTOWN

CHINATOWN

PENN QUARTER

Places to See:

1. Ronald Reagan Building and International Trade Center
2. The Old Post Office Pavilion
3. NATIONAL ARCHIVES BUILDING ★
4. Federal Trade Commission
5. Canadian Embassy
6. U.S. Navy Memorial and Navy Heritage Center
7. J. Edgar Hoover Building
8. Martin Luther King, Jr. Memorial Library
9. Jewish Historical Society of Greater Washington
10. Sixth and I Historic Synagogue
11. National Theatre
12. Warner Theatre
13. Ford's Theatre
14. Shakespeare Theatre Company
15. Woolly Mammoth Theatre Company
16. Warehouse Theatre
17. The Capitol Steps
18. International Spy Museum
19. NATIONAL PORTRAIT GALLERY/SMITHSONIAN AMERICAN ART MUSEUM ★
20. Zenith Gallery
21. Gallery at Flashpoint
22. Numark Gallery
23. Touchstone Gallery
24. Edison Place Gallery
25. Bead Museum
26. National Geographic Museum at Explorers Hall
27. National Museum of Women in the Arts
28. Goethe-Institut
29. Lillian & Albert Small Jewish Museum
30. Verizon Center
31. National Building Museum
32. Marian Koshland Science Museum

Places to Eat & Drink:

33. Le Paradou
34. Capital Grille
35. Café Atlantico

★ *Top Picks*

Where to Shop:

Where to Stay:

●●● *to Metro Center*

●● *to Federal Triangle, or McPherson Square*

●● *to Archives-Navy Memorial, or Mt. Vernon Square/7th Street-Convention Center*

● *to Farragut North*

●●● *to Gallery Place/Chinatown*

● SNAPSHOT ●

Washington's Downtown area, the heart of the Capital City, is a sprawling central business district that includes a number of museums, the well-known K Street corridor where DC lawyers work and dine, and Chinatown. Historic Penn Quarter, the revitalized part of the Downtown area, is a mix of federal buildings, notably the National Archives; a flourishing theater district; museums and galleries, including the National Portrait Gallery and the Smithsonian American Museum of Art, and the International Spy Museum; and a number of excellent places to eat. As you walk southeast on Pennsylvania Avenue, you'll note the great view of the U.S. Capitol in the distance. You'll also see federal workers hurrying to work, and tourists studying their maps. It's all part of the energy of Downtown.

There is a lot to see and do here but be prepared to walk, or plan to take the Metro or a bus. For example, ride the Metro's Yellow, Red, or Green Lines to Gallery Place-Chinatown, where the world's largest Chinese Arch, the Friendship Arch, fashioned from 7,000 pieces of glazed tile, stands at 7th Street and H, NW. From here you can also explore Washington's little Chinatown, or reach the Verizon Center and surrounding eateries.

PLACES TO SEE
Landmarks:
One of the most impressive federal buildings—for its sheer size, soaring rotunda, and arched skylight—is the **Ronald Reagan Building and International Trade Center (1)** *(1300 Pennsylvania Ave. NW, 202-312-1300 or 888-393-3306, www.itcdc.com)*. Filling two city blocks, it is home to a variety of government offices, the **DC Visitor Information Center**, which provides tickets to events, the venue of **The Capitol Steps (17)**, a musical, political satire troupe *(see page 106)*, cafés, a food court, and free, live entertainment in summer. Continue southeast on Pennsylvania Avenue to **The Old Post Office Pavilion (2)** *(1100 Pennsylvania Ave. NW, 202-289-4224, www.oldpostofficedc. com)*, an 1899 Romanesque-style U.S. Post Office. It's now a popular shopping and dining destination. Check out the view from the observation deck of the 315-foot clock tower.

See the Declaration of Independence, Constitution, Bill of Rights, Emancipation Proclamation, and the Louisiana Purchase up close at the ★NATIONAL ARCHIVES BUILDING (3) *(700 Pennsylvania Ave. NW, 202-357-5000, www.archives.gov)*. You should plan to spend at least 90 minutes at this visitor-friendly facility. First, you'll view an 11-minute introductory film in the 290-seat William G. McGowan Theater.

TOP PICK!

Then you're invited to tour the Archives' three exhibit galleries. The Lawrence F. O'Brien changing exhibit showcases specific collections of holdings, such as eyewitness accounts of key moments in American history. The Public Vaults permanent exhibit offers an insider glimpse into the stacks and vaults of the National Archives. Here, you can access more than 1,000 fascinating records, including Oval Office audio recordings and Abraham Lincoln's telegrams to his generals. New interactive exhibits also allow visitors to "touch" and explore some of the most interesting documents, photographs, and films in the Archives' holdings. The Rotunda for the Charters of Freedom is the home of the Declaration of Independence, Constitution, and Bill of Rights. Recent renovations here now make it possible for visitors to view all four pages of the Constitution, and new displays have made the three Charters more accessible for children and those using wheelchairs. In addition, the once-faded Rotunda murals of the presentation of the

Declaration of Independence and the Constitution, painted 70 years ago by artist Barry Faulkner, have been fully restored.

Note: Without reservations it may take an hour or more to enter the Archives through the general public entry, especially in the spring, over Thanksgiving weekend, and the week between Christmas and New Year's Day. You should be prepared to wait outdoors. To make a reservation, contact the Visitor Services Manager at visitorservices@nara.gov. Your visit date and time will be scheduled and a confirmation will be sent; you must present it upon entry.

Next door to the Archives, the **Federal Trade Commission (4)** *(600 Pennsylvania Ave. NW, ftc.gov)* focuses on consumer protection and anti-competitive business practices. Further east, for programs related to Canadian culture, visit the strikingly designed **Canadian Embassy (5)** *(501 Pennsylvania Ave. NW, 202-682-1740, www.canadianembassy.org)*. One of the most compelling outdoor memorials is that of the nearby **U.S. Navy Memorial and Navy Heritage Center (6)**

(701 Pennsylvania Ave. NW, 202-737-2300, www.lonesailor.org), which features a 100-foot granite map of the world and a seven-foot statue of the *Lone Sailor*. Bronze for the statue was mixed with artifacts from U.S. Navy ships, including the U.S.S. *Constitution* ("Old Ironsides"). Official ceremonies

and outdoor concerts draw locals and visitors. The **J. Edgar Hoover Building (7)** *(935 Pennsylvania Ave. NW, 202-324-3447)* is home to the

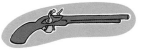

Federal Bureau of Investigation. Tour highlights include seeing a crime lab, a practice firing range, and viewing the current Ten Most Wanted Fugitives. As of this writing, however, the building is closed to the public for renovations, and is scheduled to reopen in spring 2007. Check www.fbi.gov/about us/tour for current information.

Follow H Street east to the **Martin Luther King, Jr. Memorial Library (8)** *(901 G St. NW, 202-727-1111, www.dclibrary.org/mlk)*, the only DC building designed by modern master Ludwig Mies van der Rohe. A mural by Don Miller depicts Dr. King's life and the history of the Civil Rights movement. The nearby **Jewish Historical Society of Greater Washington (9)** *(600 I St. NW, 202-789-0900, www.jhsgw.org)* is located in a restored 1876 synagogue. The **Sixth and I Historic Synagogue (10)** *(600 I St. NW, 202-408-3100, www. sixthandi.org)*, another restored sanctuary, houses two Torah scrolls that survived the Holocaust.

Arts & Entertainment:

Don't miss the quality offerings of Washingon's thriving theater district. It's the place for avant-garde productions as well as national touring musicals. The **National Theatre (11)** *(1321 Pennsylvania Ave. NW, 202-628-6161,* *www.nationaltheatre.org)* features tours of Broadway shows, pre-Broadway shows, and American premieres. The **Warner Theatre (12)** *(513 13th St. NW, 202-783-4000, www.warnertheatre.com)* hosts Broadway productions, comedies, dance performances, films, and concerts. You'll love its marble and gilded-gold lobby and chandelier-lit auditorium. **Ford's Theatre (13)** *(511 10th St. NW, 202-347-4833, www.fordstheatre.org)* is the place where actor John Wilkes Booth shot Abraham Lincoln on April 14, 1865. Talks on the theater's history are presented throughout the day. Self-guided tours are available. The renowned **Shakespeare Theatre Company (14)** *(450 7th St. NW, 202-547-1122, www. shakespearetheatre.org)* has been called "the nation's foremost Shakespeare company" by the *Wall Street Journal*. The **Woolly Mammoth Theatre Company (15)** *(641 D St. NW, 202-393-3939, www.woollymammoth. net)* performs and premieres experimental plays by emerging writers. **Warehouse Theater (16)** *(1021 7th St.

NW, 202-783-3933, www. warehousetheater.com)*, called "an avant-garde Kennedy Center" by the *Washington Post*, produces some of the city's edgiest plays; it also has an art gallery, café, music venue, and film screening room. Featuring musical political satire, **The Capitol Steps (17)** *(Ronald Reagan Building, 13th and Pennsylvania Ave. NW, 202-312-1555, www.capsteps. com)*, made up of Capitol Hill staffers, performs Fridays and Saturdays at 7:30 PM.

Museums to investigate include the **International Spy Museum (18)** *(800 F St. NW, 202-393-7798, www.spymuseum.org)*, home to the world's largest collection of inter-

national espionage artifacts, from concealment devices, sabotage weapons, and cipher machines to dead drops, secret writings, and microdots.

Two newly renovated Smithsonian museums are here, too: The ★**NATIONAL PORTRAIT GALLERY (19)**, with its thousands of images of American citizens, strives to present "history with personality," while the ★**SMITHSONIAN AMERICAN ART MUSEUM (19)** *(8th/F Sts. NW, www.npg. si.edu and www.smithsonian.org)* showcases the works of American artists at their best. Both museums are located in the former Patent Office, one of DC's oldest public buildings. This acclaimed Greek Revival structure, with its double curving staircase and two city-block-long sky-lights, dates from 1836, when it was the home of the U.S. Patent Office. A total renovation of this landmark was completed in 2006.

TOP PICK!

The **National Portrait Gallery (19)** collection includes thousands of the world's most compelling paintings, sculptures, drawings, and photographs of notable Americans, from the famous "Lansdowne" portrait of George Washington and the "cracked plate" portrait of Abraham Lincoln to portraits of Babe Ruth, Rosa Parks, Marilyn Monroe, and a striking photograph of Shaquille O'Neal.

The **Smithsonian American Art Museum (19)** is home to the first U.S. federal art collection. Its holdings include colonial portraiture, 19th-century landscapes, American impressionism, 20th-century realism and abstraction, New Deal projects, sculpture, photography, contemporary crafts, and African American, Latino, and folk art. More than 7,000 American artists are represented, including Winslow Homer, John Singer Sargent, Childe Hassam, Georgia O'Keeffe, Edward Hopper, Robert Rauschenberg, Nam June Paik, and Martin Puryear.

You'll also want to stop by the museums' **Lunder Conservation Center**; this unique facility allows you to observe conservators caring for the museums' national treasures through floor-to-ceiling windows. The Luce Foundation for American Art is the first visible art storage and study center, and affords visitors access to 3,300 additional museum pieces.

You'll also find a cluster of art galleries spotlighting local and national artists, including **Zenith Gallery (20)** *(413 7th St. NW, 202-783-2963, www.zenithgallery.com)*, **Gallery at Flashpoint (21)** *(916 G St. NW, 202-315-1310, www.flashpointdc.org)*, **Numark Gallery (22)** *(625-627 E St. NW, 202-628-3810, www.numarkgallery.com)*, **Touchstone Gallery (23)** *(406 7th St. NW, 202-347-2787, www.touchstonegallery.com)*, and the **Edison Place Gallery (24)** *(702 8th St. NW, 202-872-3391, www.pepco.com)*, a 4,100-square-foot space, located in the Pepco headquarters building.

The intriguing **Bead Museum (25)** *(400 7th St. NW, 202-624-4500, www.beadmuseumdc.org)* examines beads as both artifacts and objects of beauty; its "Bead Timeline" displays 2,000 beads chronologically. In the Farragut North Metro stop vicinity, visit the **National Geographic Museum at Explorers Hall (26)** *(1145 17th St. NW, 202-857-7588, www.nationalgeographic.com/ museum)* to see the magazine come alive through changing exhibits. The interactive displays and video touch-screens allow you to experience a mini-tornado to a trip around the world. In the McPherson Square Metro stop area, the **National Museum of Women in the Arts (27)** *(1250 New York Ave. NW, 202-783-5000 or 800-222-7270, www.nmwa.org)* showcases more than 3,000 works by women artists dating from the 16th century to the present. See works by Mary Cassatt, Georgia O'Keeffe, and Louise Nevelson. At the **Goethe-Institut (28)** *(812 7th St. NW, 202-289-1200, www.goethe.de/washington)*, a Federal Republic of Germany cultural center shows films and runs discussions and language classes. The **Lillian & Albert Small Jewish Museum (29)** *(corner of 3rd and G Sts. NW, by appointment only)* is dedicated to the story of the local Jewish community and features a restored sanctuary. The **Verizon Center (30)** *(601 F St. NW, 202-628-3200, www.verizoncenter.com)* (formerly the MCI Center), a state-of-the-art sports and entertainment complex, is home to NBA's Washington Wizards, the NHL's Washington Capitals, the WNBA's Washington Mystics, and the Georgetown Hoyas men's basketball team. If you're interested in architecture, design, and engineering, don't miss the **National Building Museum (31)** *(401 F St. NW, 202-272-2448, www.nbm.org, free admission)*, located in a stunning red brick building. Its main interior hall features 75-foot Corinthian columns that are among the tallest in the world. To learn about the latest scientific research, including global warming and DNA analysis, stop by the **Marian Koshland Science Museum (32)** *(6th and E Sts. NW, 202-334-1201, www.koshland-science-museum.org)*, operated by the National Academy of Sciences. Recommended for children over the age of 13.

PLACES TO EAT & DRINK
Where to Eat:

For lively dining with plenty of variety, the Downtown area fills the bill. **Le Paradou (33)** *($$-$$$)* *(678 Indiana Ave. NW, 202-347-6780, www.leparadou.net)* features contemporary French cuisine in elegant surroundings. Whether you choose lobster or Black Angus filet, it's a memorable experience. The **Capital Grille (34)** *($$$)* *(601 Pennsylvania Ave. NW, 202-737-6200, www.thecapital grille.com)*, is known for its dry aged steaks, seafood, and chops, accompanied by acclaimed service. For tasty, creative Mexican, Latin American, and Spanish fare, **Café Atlantico (35)** *($$)* *(405 8th St. NW, 202-393-0812, www.cafeatlantico.com)* is a Washington favorite for its innovative Nuevo Latin-style food and guacamole, prepared at your table. For masala crab cakes, ginger scallops, or Indian barbecue, where you can watch the chef in action, reserve a seat at

Rasika (36) ($$) *(633 D St. NW, 202-637-1222, www.rasikarestaurant.com)*; its name is derived from a Sanskrit word for "flavors." The **Hard Rock Café (37) ($$)** *(999 E. St. NW, 202-737-7625, www.hardrockcafe.com)* has an outpost here, too. **TenPenh (38) ($$)** *(1001 Pennsylvania Ave. NW, 202-393-4500, www.tenpenh.com)* presents some of the tastiest Southeast Asian food in Washington, from red Thai curry shrimp to pecan-crusted halibut to lemongrass custard cake. For a quick pick-me-up, consider **Teaism (39) ($)** *(400 8th St. NW, 202-638-6010, www.teaism.com)*, serving specialty teas, cookies, and Pan-Asian treats, including bento boxes with teriyaki salmon, vegetable tempura, chicken, and other choices. For a menu of more than 60 hot or cold tapas, **Jaleo (40) ($$)** *(480 7th St. NW, 202-628-7949, www.jaleo.com)* delivers. Its name means "merrymaking" in Spanish—stop by on a Wednesday night when the Sevillanas dancers perform. **Andale (41) ($-$$)** *(401 7th St. NW, 202-783-3133, www.andaledc.com)* offers unexpected variations on Mexican favorites and great-tasting margaritas. Sip a "spy-tini" as you snoop on your neighboring diners (or the chef) through strategically placed portholes at **Zola (42) ($$-$$$)** *(800 F St. NW, 202-654-0999 www.zoladc.com)*, named for the French novelist Émile Zola. Red velvet booths and art made from declassified CIA documents add to the intriguing style.

Menu items include prawns, grilled veal, or lobster roll. For a quick meal, the **Spy City Café (43) ($)** *(800 F St. NW, 202-654-0995, www.zoladc.com)* offers homemade soups, sandwiches, and pizza. **Zaytinya (44) ($$-$$$)** *(701 9th St. NW, 202-638-0800, www.zaytinya.com)* offers a flavorful array of Greek, Turkish, and Lebanese *mezze* (appetizers). For dessert, try the Turkish coffee chocolate cake. **Austin Grill (45) ($)** *(750 E. St. NW, 202-393-3776, www.austingrill.com)* is a branch of the popular Washington area restaurant that rustles up reliable, reasonable Tex-Mex food in a lively atmosphere. Within the **Ronald Reagan Building and International Trade Center (1)**, **Aria Trattoria (46) ($)** *(1300 Pennsylvania Ave. NW, 202-312-1250, www.ariatrattoria.com)* is an inviting indoor/outdoor trattoria offering homemade pasta,

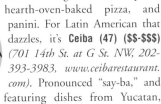

hearth-oven-baked pizza, and panini. For Latin American that dazzles, it's **Ceiba (47) ($$-$$$)** *(701 14th St. at G St. NW, 202-393-3983, www.ceibarestaurant.com)*. Pronounced "say-ba," and featuring dishes from Yucatan, Brazilian, Peruvian, and Cuban traditions, the acclaimed restaurant is decorated in shades of cocoa brown, burnt red, ice blue, and sage green. **DC Coast Restaurant (48) ($$-$$$)** *(1401 K St. NW, 202-216-5988, www.dccoast.com)* with a lively Art Deco bar, serves modern American cuisine with a Gulf Coast influence. Try the seafood gumbo or Chinese-style smoked lobster. **Coeur de Lion (49) ($$-$$$)** *(Henley Park Hotel, 926 Massachusetts Ave. NW, 202-414-0500)* is a romantic haven for elegant dining under crystal chandeliers. The menu of this top-rated restaurant combines fresh seafood, seasonal ingredients, and market finds. The popular **District Chop House (50) ($$-$$$)** *(509 7th St. at E St. NW, 202-347-3434, www.chophouse.com)* is located less than a block from the Verizon Center. Sample a beer from its on-site brewery. Enjoy a steak or brick-oven pizza. A full-service Scotch and bourbon bar, billiard tables, and cigar lounge will round out your experience here. The **Morrison-Clark (51) ($$-$$$)** *(Massachusetts Ave. and 11th St. NW, 202-898-1200, www. morrisonclark.com)*, with its marble fireplaces, gilded mirrors, and lace curtains, offers an elegant, 19th-century setting. Dine alfresco in its brick courtyard. The American/Continental menu is imbued with Southern flavor. For true Louisiana-style cuisine, **Acadiana (52) ($$)** *(901 New York Ave. NW, 202-408-8848, www.acadianarestaurant.com)* is the place. Its New Orleans–style barbecue shrimp was named a *USA Today* "Top 25 Dish" for 2005. The **Oceanaire Seafood Room (53) ($$$)** *(1201 F St. NW, 202-347-BASS, www. oceanaire.com)*, a sumptuous seafood restaurant reminiscent of a 1930s ocean liner, serves the freshest seafood in town. Flown in daily, grilled or broiled choices are the main event here and vary depending on the day's catch. For Tuscan-style Italian prepared in an open-air kitchen, choose **Tuscana West (54) ($$)** *(1350 I St., 13th/14th Sts. NW, 202-289-7300, www.tuscanawest.net)*.

Café Promenade (55) ($$-$$$) *(Renaissance Mayflower Hotel, 1127 Connecticut Ave. NW, 202-347-2233)* serves classic Mediterranean dishes from Greece, Spain, and Italy. Try elegant afternoon tea or the champagne  Sunday brunch. In the compact environs of Chinatown, you'll find a number of Cantonese, Szechuan, Hunan, and Mongolian eateries. **Full Kee (56) ($)** *(509 H St. NW, 202-371-2233)* is a local favorite for its satisfying menu and affordable prices. Try its wonton soup, dumplings, hot pot, and noodles.

Bars & Nightlife:

You'll find four levels of entertainment at **RNR Bar and Lounge (57)** *(717 6th St. NW, 202-589-0016, www.rnrdc.com)*, including two floors for dancing, live music and DJs, big-screen plasma TVs, and a rooftop patio bar. **ESPN Zone (58)** *(555 12th St. NW, 202-783-3776, www.espnzone.com)* is for sports fans of all ages. Interactive games, 200 TVs, a bar, and a screening room with a 16-foot video screen make this a fun place to eat burgers and fries. **Fado (59)** *(808 7th St. NW, 202-789-0066, www.fadoirishpub.com)* is an Irish pub in the midst of Chinatown. Just about every element of its decor—from the stones in the floor to the etched wood—was imported from Ireland. Celtic rock shows, trivia nights, and menu choices like corned beef and cabbage will make you feel as if you've been transported to the land of the leprechaun. A mecca for the young and beautiful, **Platinum (60)** *(915 F St. NW, 202-393-*

3555, *www.platinumclubdc.com*) nightclub is housed in an antique building with original marble floors. It boasts three dance floors and a VIP lounge. **Polly Esther's (61)** *(605 12th St. NW, 202-737-1970, www.polyesthers.com)*, another dance club, features '70s disco music on one level and '80s tunes on another; "Club Expo" on the third, blasts current radio hits. Four DJs keep the upscale crowd moving and shaking at **Home (62)** *(911 F St. NW, 202-638-4663)*, a 10,000-square-foot, five-floor former bank. Its happy hour offers reduced drink prices and a complimentary buffet.

WHERE TO SHOP

Gallery Place (63) *(7th and H Sts. NW)* is home to a 14-screen Regal Cinema, Ann Taylor, Urban Outfitters, Häagen-Dazs, and Aveda, among others. At **Fahrney's (64)** *(1317 F St. NW, 202-628-9525, www.fahrneyspens.com)*, established in 1929, you can buy fine writing instruments, stationery, gifts, and desk accessories. With its selection of poetry, literary fiction, and foreign-language literature, **Chapters (65)** *(445 11th St. NW, 202-737-5553, www.chaptersliterary.com)* attracts serious readers and inveterate browsers. **Filene's Basement (66)** *(1133 Connecticut Ave. NW at DeSales St., 202-872-8430, filenesbasement.com)* is bargain central for clothing and all sorts of accessories.

WHERE TO STAY

The **Courtyard by Marriott–Convention Center (67)** ($$-$$$) *(900 F St. NW, 202-638-4600 or 800-321-2211, www.courtyard.com/wascn)*, a restored historic landmark, is a comfortable, convenient place to stay. It's across from the **International Spy Museum (18)** and a block from the **Verizon Center (30)**. **Hotel Harrington (68)** ($) *(436 11th St. NW, 202-628-8140 or 800-424-8532, www.hotel-harrington.com)* is a friendly, family-owned hotel that's convenient to museums, theaters, and the Old Post Office Pavilion; it offers 26 deluxe family rooms. For luxury with a twist, book the vibrant, historic **Hotel Monaco (69)** ($$$) *(700 F St. NW, 202-628-7177, www.monaco-dc.com)*; your stay includes "Guppy Love," a companion goldfish to keep you company. (Housekeeping cares for your finned friend.) The **Renaissance Mayflower Hotel (70)** ($$$) *(1127 Connecticut Ave., 202-347-3000 or 800-228-7697, www.renaissancehotels.com)* is one of the largest, most historic, and loveliest hotels in Washington. Calvin Coolidge's inaugural ball took place here. Want to be in the heart of the city, close to the Convention Center? Stay at the **Grand Hyatt Washington (71)** ($$-$$$) *(1000 H St. NW, 202-582-1234 or 800-223-1234, www.grandwashington.hyatt.com)*; it features a soaring atrium, a "lagoon," a 35-foot waterfall, six restaurants and bars, and access to the Metro Center. Enter another era at the **Henley Park Hotel (72)** ($$-$$$) *(926 Massachusetts Ave. NW, 202-638-5200 or 800-222-8474, www.henleypark.com)*, a restored Tudor-style hotel with gargoyles, leaded windows, Edwardian furnishings, and "white-glove" service. It's located one block from the Convention Center. Tea is served daily at 4:00 PM. The **Morrison-Clark Inn (73) ($-$$$)** *(Massachusetts Ave. and 11th St. NW, 202-898-1200 or 800-222-8474, www.morrisonclark.com)* is comprised of two Victorian town houses. **The Jefferson (74) ($$$)** *(1200 16th St. NW, 202-347-2200 or 866-270-8120, www.thejeffersonwashingtondc.com)*, a metropolitan boutique hotel, showcases original documents signed by Jefferson and offers romantic, residential-style accommodations four blocks from the White House.

chapter 5

UPPER NORTHWEST
AND ENVIRONS

ADAMS MORGAN

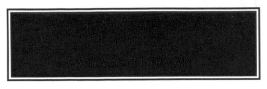

UPPER NORTHWEST AND ENVIRONS
ADAMS MORGAN

Places to See:

1. Fort Reno Park
2. Rock Creek Park
3. Klingle Mansion
4. Kennedy-Warren Apartment Building
5. WASHINGTON NATIONAL CATHEDRAL ★
6. Islamic Center
7. National Zoological Park
8. Rock Creek Park's Nature Center and Planetarium
9. Rock Creek Park Horse Center
10. Uptown Theater
11. Avalon Theatre
12. Hillwood Museum & Gardens
37. Three Macaws Mural
38. Latin American Youth Center and Latino Community Heritage Center
39. Cows on a Bicycle Mural
40. Patricia M. Sitar Center for the Arts
41. Toulouse-Lautrec Mural
42. Madam's Organ Mural
43. District of Columbia Arts Center
44. Champorama Park Mural
45. Meridian Hill Park

Places to Eat & Drink:

13. The Dancing Crab/ The Malt Shop
14. New Heights
15. Lebanese Taverna
16. Ardeo/Bardeo
17. Lavandou
18. Indique
19. Booeymonger
20. Mazza Café
21. Café Olé
22. Cactus Cantina
23. Café Deluxe
24. Bambule
46. Mama Ayesha's Restaurant
47. Meskerem
48. The Grill from Ipanema
49. Cashion's Eat Place
50. Mixtec
51. Perry's
52. Pasta Mia
53. Felix/The Spy Lounge
54. Habana Village

★ *Top Picks*

Washington is a very easy city for you
to forget where you came from and
why you got there in the first place.

—*Harry S. Truman*

● *to Woodley Park-Zoo/Adams Morgan,*
  or Cleveland Park, or Van Ness/UDC,
  or Tenleytown/AU, or Friendship Heights

● **SNAPSHOT** ●

Upper Northwest—located northwest of the nearly 1,800 acres of Rock Creek Park—offers several interesting places to see, including the National Zoo, Washington National Cathedral, and the Hillwood Museum and Gardens. Popular restaurants dot Connecticut and Wisconsin Avenues. Rock Creek Park dates back to 1866, when a Senate committee sought to locate an attractive tract of land for the presidential mansion. Though the chief executive's home was never resituated here, the park became a place of respite and relaxation for locals and visitors alike. Park-goers enjoy cycling, golfing, picnicking, horseback riding, or wandering through the area's natural beauty.

Rock Creek Parkway wends its way through the park, offering motorists lovely scenic views. Most places of interest in Upper Northwest are accessible by Metro. Some call Connecticut Avenue a "corridor," and it is an appropriate description, as nearby attractions are like

"rooms" situated off it. Determine your priorities, then take the Metro to the appropriate stop. For example, to visit the Zoo, use the Woodley Park-Zoo/Adams Morgan stop and walk up Connecticut Avenue. Or use the Cleveland Park stop and walk downhill.

PLACES TO SEE
Landmarks:
Fort Reno Park (1) *(Chesapeake St. and Nebraska Ave. NW, 202-521-1493, www.fortreno.com)* is the highest point in DC, and was once used as a Civil War fort. Its free summer concerts are a Washington tradition. The most striking feature of Upper Northwest, however, is **Rock Creek Park (2)** *(Beach Drive NW)*, a tranquil oasis in the capital city. The park also contains Civil War–era ruins, a nature center and planetarium, and the **Carter Barron Amphitheatre**. Wildlife abounds—don't be surprised if you catch a glimpse of deer, coyotes, foxes, or beavers. There are numerous entrances to Rock Creek, including the one at the **Klingle Mansion (3)** *(3545 Williamsburg Ln. NW, 202-895-6070, www.nps.gov/rocr)*, a large stone farmhouse built in 1823 that serves as the park's headquarters. Outside Rock Creek, in the Cleveland Park Historic District, you'll find a number of landmarks near the Cleveland Park Metro stop, including historic mansions that were once summer retreats. The **Kennedy-Warren Apartment Building (4)** *(3133 Connecticut Ave.*

NW) is a renowned Aztec/Art Deco masterpiece that has been home to a variety of distinguished residents, among them Lyndon B. and "Lady Bird" Johnson, author P. J. O'Rourke, and during World War II, numerous generals and admirals.

The ★WASHINGTON NATIONAL CATHEDRAL (5) *(Massachusetts and Wisconsin Aves. NW, 202-537-6200, www.nationalcathedral.org; 30-minute guided tours available, call 202-364-6616),* officially known as the Cathedral Church of St. Peter and St. Paul, has served as the site for major services, such as George W. Bush's inaugural prayer service and Ronald Reagan's state funeral. Martin Luther King, Jr. preached his last Sunday sermon from its pulpit on March 31, 1968; he was assassinated four days later. Helen Keller and her tutor Annie Sullivan are buried here, as is Woodrow Wilson. Though affiliated with the Episcopal Church, its doors are open to all faiths.

Nearly the length of two football fields, the massive limestone structure is the second largest cathedral in the U.S. and the sixth largest in the world. Its central, 300-foot Gloria in Excelsis Tower is the highest point in the District of Columbia. Seventy windows in the seventh-floor Pilgrim Observation Gallery provide panoramic views. Designed by leading British Gothic architect George Frederick Bodley after medieval cathedrals, this 20th-century architectural marvel features flying buttresses, 215 stained-glass windows, 110 gargoyles, and a 53-bell carillon.

TOP PICK!

The cathedral's cornerstone, which came from the Bethlehem region, was inset into a larger piece of American granite. It was laid by Theodore Roosevelt and the Bishop of London in 1907; construction was completed in 1990. The cathedral's high altar is made from stones quarried near Jerusalem. The pulpit is constructed from stones from Canterbury Cathedral, and the stone for the bishop's formal seat, or cathedra (the origin of the word "cathedral"), comes from ancient Glastonbury Abbey. You'll find the cathedral filled with American commemoratives, such as statues of Washington and Lincoln, state flags, floor-inlaid state seals, and stained-glass windows depicting special achievements, such as the Lewis and Clark expedition. The Space Window honors man's landing on the moon, and even includes a fragment of lunar rock!

Don't miss the cathedral's intriguing gargoyles and grotesques, including a boar, a braying donkey, a cat, a dog, and Darth Vader. For a colorful and fragrance-filled interlude, stop at the cathedral's Herb Cottage or stroll the medieval Bishop's Garden. Handouts are provided for self-guided tours. Or take advantage of the cathedral's variety of specialized tours, from gargoyle tours and tea tours to garden tours and woodland walks, spotlighting the cathedral's 57 acres of grounds on Mount Saint Alban. Tour fee donations support the cathedral's programs and ministry. Call 202-364-6616 for a weekly listing. The cathedral is 1-1/2 miles from the Tenleytown–AU Metro stop on the Red Line. Or take the #30, #32, #34, or #36 bus south.

Arts & Entertainment:

The **Islamic Center (6)** *(2551 Massachusetts Ave. NW, 202-332-8343, www.theislamiccenter.com)* is located in a white limestone building topped with a 160-foot minaret. It's filled with art from the Middle East, including Persian carpets and stained-glass windows. It also contains a library and hosts lectures.

The **National Zoological Park (7)** *(3001 Connecticut Ave. NW, 202-673-4800, www.natzoo.si.edu)*, or more simply, the National Zoo, is an ideal place for the entire family. Visit the Giant Panda Habitat to see Mei Xiang and Tian Tian, on loan from China until 2010, and their cub Tai Shan. You may need timed tickets for viewing; check the zoo's Web site. For early risers, the zoo's grounds open at 6:00 AM. (Buildings open at 10:00 AM.) **Rock Creek Park's Nature Center and Planetarium (8)**

(Rock Creek Park, 5200 Glover Rd. NW, 202-895-6070) is another great place for kids. There are guided walks on weekends, the hands-on Discovery Room, and a planetarium. The **Rock Creek Park Horse Center (9)** *(5100 Glover Rd. NW, 202-362-0117, www.rockcreek horsecenter.com)* next door offers guided trail rides. Like outdoor entertainment? **Carter Barron Amphitheatre** in upper Rock Creek *(4850 Colorado Ave. NW, 202-426-0486, www.nps.gov/rocr)* hosts Shakespeare and other productions and concerts all summer long in a

4,200-seat venue with outstanding natural acoustics. The largest movie screen in DC can be found at the Art Deco **Uptown Theater (10)** *(3426 Connecticut Ave. NW, 202-966-5400, http://cinematreasures.org)*. Opened in 1933, it underwent a major renovation in 1996, including the addition of a 300–stadium seat balcony. The **Avalon Theatre (11)** *(5612 Connecticut Ave. NW, just south of Chevy Chase Cir., 202-966-6000, www.theavalon.org)*, a historic landmark, has been a popular gathering place for families since 1923, especially after air-conditioning was installed in 1937. It now shows foreign, independent, and documentary films. Closer to the Van Ness–UDC Metro stop, you'll spot the stately **Hillwood Museum & Gardens (12)** *(4155 Linnean Ave. NW, Upton/Tilden Sts., 202-686-5807; reservations req., call 877-HILLWOOD; closed Jan. and national holidays, www.hillwoodmuseum.org)*. The restored estate of Marjorie Merriweather Post, heiress to the Post cereal fortune, Hillwood comprises 25 landscaped acres and a 40-room mansion filled with treasures she collected throughout the world, including Fabergé pieces and

18th- and 19th-century French furnishings. Outside, you can stroll through Mrs. Post's Japanese-style garden, rose garden, and formal French Parterre Garden. Walking further north, you'll pass the **Walter Reed Army Medical Center**. Located on the grounds is the **National**

Museum of Health and Medicine *(6900 Georgia Ave., 202-782-2200, www.nmhm.washingtondc.museum)*. The facility was founded in 1862 to research medical conditions that arose during the Civil War. Today it displays human specimens, photographs of amputations, and medical instruments. It also includes historical artifacts from Lincoln's assassination.

PLACES TO EAT & DRINK
Where to Eat:

The Dancing Crab (13) ($$) *(4611 Wisconsin Ave. NW, 202-244-1882, www.dancingcrab.com)* is a casual, fun place to go for fresh crabs. Brown-paper tablecloths, paper towels, and mallets are the order of the day. Stand-out eateries in Woodley Park include **New Heights (14) ($$$)** *(2317 Calvert St. NW, 202-234-4110, www.newheightsrestaurant.com)*, offering New American cuisine. Try pan-roasted red snapper with braised fennel, lamb curry, or black bean pâté. Popular **Lebanese Taverna (15) ($$)** *(2641 Connecticut Ave. NW, 202-265-8681, www.lebanesetaverna.com)* is tops in the family category with its tempting, value-priced menu and fresh bread baked on premises in a wood-burning oven. Near the Cleveland Park Metro stop, dine with politicos and media at acclaimed **Ardeo/Bardeo (16) ($$$)** *(3309 Connecticut Ave. NW, 202-244-6750, www. ardeorestaurant.com)*, a neighborhood restaurant known for its modern American menu, incorporating Asian and Mediterranean influences in a sleek, art-filled setting. For classic French food, choose **Lavandou (17)** **($$$)** *(3321 Connecticut Ave. NW, 202-966-3003, www. lavandourestaurant.net).* **Indique (18) ($-$$)** *(3512-14 Connecticut Ave. NW, 202-244-6600, www.indique. com)* prepares Indian food with new twists on dishes like Cornish game hen, served in a paste of curry leaves and hot peppers. Crowd-pleasing **Booeymonger (19) ($)**

(5252 Wisconsin Ave. NW, 202-686-5805, www.booeymonger.com), near the Friendship Heights Metro stop, has been turning out specialty sandwiches and wraps for more than 30 years. Kids' menu is also available. Sip a fresh-brewed coffee, an espresso, or a cappuccino at **Mazza Café (20)** *(Mazza Gallerie, 5300 N. Wisconsin Ave. NW, 202-244-3331, www. mazzagallerie.com).*

If you're driving, check out the restaurants clustered along Wisconsin Avenue a block or two from the **Washington National Cathedral (5).** For *mezzes,* tapas, and other Mediterranean dishes, accompanied by a microbrew, a glass of wine, or a martini, choose **Café Olé (21) ($)** *(4000 Wisconsin Ave. NW, 202-244-1330, www. cafeoledc.com).* **Cactus Cantina (22) ($)** *(3300 Wisconsin Ave. NW, 202-682-7222, www.cactuscantina.com)* serves up tasty Tex/Mex classics that families—presidential and otherwise—will love.

Bars & Nightlife

The Malt Shop (13) *(4611 Wisconsin Ave. NW, 202-244-9733)* on the second floor of **The Dancing Crab** is a local favorite sports bar, where there is always a game on the TV to watch as you drink a beer. For a well-rounded menu—from chicken pot pie to grilled salmon niçoise salad—and a tavernlike setting that incorporates leather booths, a mahogany bar, and white tablecloths, head to **Café Deluxe (23)** *(3228 Wisconsin Ave. NW, 202-686-2233, www.cafedeluxe.com)*. Enjoy the cozy atmosphere at **Bambule (24)** *(5225 Wisconsin Ave. NW, 202-966-0300, www.bambuledc.com)* as  you nibble on the various tapas and partake of the Mediterranean cuisine. Weekend evenings there's a DJ playing festive international and Latin music.

WHERE TO SHOP

For more than two decades, Politics & Prose Bookstore and Coffeehouse (25) *(5015 Connecticut Ave. NW, 202-364-1919 or 800-722-0790, www.politics-prose.com)* has been the place to go for browsing, buying, and author events. Near the Friendship Heights Metro stop, you'll find a number of upscale shopping malls and free-standing stores, including Mazza Gallerie (26) *(5300 N. Wisconsin Ave. NW, 202-966-6114, www.mazzagallerie.com)*, home to AMC theaters, Neiman Marcus, Saks Fifth Avenue Men's Store, Williams-Sonoma, Pampillonia Jewelers, Chas Schwartz & Son, Filene's Basement, and Harriet Kassman, which offers

designer clothing for women. The **Chevy Chase Pavilion (27)** *(5335 Wisconsin Ave. NW, 202-686-5335, www.ccpavilion.com)* across the street offers another collection of shops, including Pottery Barn, Talbots, Ann Taylor Loft, J. Crew, World Market, luggage store Bon Voyage, and Alpaca International, carrying women's clothes from Europe and Peru. There is also a branch of the Parisian upscale contemporary furniture store **Roche Bobois (28)** *(Chevy Chase Plaza, 5301 Wisconsin Ave. NW, 202-966-4490, www. roche-bobois.com).* **Elizabeth Arden Salon (29)** *(5225 Wisconsin Ave. NW, 202-362-9890, www.reddoorsalons. com)* provides salon and spa services. For fashions with American style, shop **Lord & Taylor (30)** *(5255 Western Ave. NW, 202-362-9600, lordandtaylor.com).* Want something different? **Wake Up Little Suzie (31)** *(3409 Connecticut Ave. NW, 202-244-0700)* is famous for its fun and fanciful gifts, including cat- and dog-shaped alarm clocks, unique pottery, and handcrafted jewelry.

WHERE TO STAY

One of the most elegant places to stay in the area is the **Omni Shoreham Hotel (32)** *($$-$$$) (2500 Calvert St. at Connecticut Ave. NW, 202-234-0700 or 888-444-6664, www.omnishorehamhotel.com).* The hotel is situated on 11 acres in Rock Creek Park; many of its rooms offer scenic views. The Omni has hosted inaugural balls for every administration since FDR's. Bolder guests are known to book its "haunted ghost suite." The **Marriott**

Wardman Park Hotel (33) ($$-$$$) *(2660 Woodley Rd. NW, 202-328-2000 or 800-228-9290, www.marriott. com/wasdt)*, the site of larger conventions, is set on a private 16-acre estate convenient to the Woodley Park-Zoo/Adams Morgan Metro stop. For a homey alternative to convention hotels, consider the Woodley Park Guest House (34) ($$) *(2647 Woodley Rd. NW, 202-667-0218 or 866-667-0218, www.woodleyparkguesthouse. com)*. This charming B&B is TV and radio-free (though it does provide guest phones, voice mail, and high-speed Internet access). A generous "continental-plus" breakfast awaits you each morning. Kalorama Guest House at Woodley Park (35) ($) *(2700 Cathedral Ave. NW, 202-328-0860, www.kaloramaguesthouse.com)*, made up of two Victorian town houses, provides comfy accommodations at inviting prices. Continental breakfast included. Embassy Suites at Chevy Chase Pavilion (36) ($$) *(Chevy Chase Pavilion, 5335 Wisconsin Ave. NW, 202-686-5335, www.ccpavilion.com/hotels)* offers complimentary breakfast and has a health and swim club.

● *to Woodley Park-Zoo/Adams Morgan—to Metro bus*

● SNAPSHOT ●

Adams Morgan is one of the liveliest and most diverse neighborhoods in the Washington area. It's filled with edgy clubs, funky shops, and the famous colorful murals that brighten the façades of the buildings along Columbia Road and 18th Street. Adams Morgan attracts the young, the hip, and the adventurous, especially at night, when its clubs resonate with blues, jazz, rock, soul, bluegrass, and Latin music. International eateries abound: Choose from Mexican, Brazilian, Turkish, Italian, Middle Eastern, Ethiopian, French, Japanese, Vietnamese, El Salvadoran, Jewish, Greek, Pan Asian, Indian, and all-American diner food, too. If avant-garde fashions, emerging designers, and offbeat furnishings intrigue you, you'll love Adams Morgan. You'll also like it if you're in search of something beyond official Washington. Stop by on the second Sunday in September, when the Adams Morgan Day Festival is in full swing. Artisans, food vendors, musicians, and dancers turn the area into a mélange of sights, scents, and flavors. Take the Metro here and walk across the Duke Ellington Bridge.

PLACES TO SEE
Arts & Entertainment

Stroll from the Metro stop east into Adams Morgan; you'll feel the pulse of the neighborhood on Columbia Road and 18th Street NW. A walking tour of Adams Morgan murals will acquaint you  with the history and culture of this unique community. The **Three Macaws Mural (37)** *(1706 Columbia Rd. NW)*, for example, is said to symbolize the neighborhood's ethnic diversity. Exhibits at the **Latin American Youth Center and Latino Community Heritage Center (38)** *(1419 Columbia Rd. NW, 14th/15th Sts., 202-319-2225, www.layc-dc.org)* tell the immigrant story through personal recollections and images. The popular **Cows on a Bicycle Mural (39)** *(2501 Champlain St. NW)*, by Sara Lee Terrat, sparked a community legal brouhaha 15 years ago. The **Patricia M. Sitar Center for the Arts (40)** *(1700 Kalorama Rd. NW, 202-797-2145, www.sitarcenter.org)* provides a place for neighborhood at-risk children, their families, and the community at large to explore music, dance, drama, writing, and visual arts. The **Toulouse-Lautrec Mural (41)** *(2461 18th St. NW)* depicts the late 19th-century Parisian artist. The eye-catching **Madam's Organ Mural (42)** *(2461 18th St. NW)* is perhaps the best-known—and most controversial—of the Adams Morgan public works of art. The **District of Columbia Arts Center (43)** *(2438 18th St. Columbia/Belmont Rds. NW, 202-462-7833, www.dcartscenter.org)* provides a gallery and a 50-seat theater for emerging local, national, and international visual and performing artists. The **Champorama Park Mural (44)** *(corner of Champlain and Kalorama Rd. NW)* was commissioned to revitalize an abandoned lot. A bench in this little pocket park provides a place for quiet reflection. Two blocks east you'll find a revitalized DC gem, the 12-acre **Meridian Hill Park (45)** *(2330 15th St. NW, 202-462-7275, www.washingtonparks.net)*, unofficially known as Malcolm X Park. It features a cascading water stairway, formal, Italian-style landscaping, and statues of Joan of Arc, Dante, and James Buchanan.

PLACES TO EAT & DRINK
Where to Eat:
Mama Ayesha's Restaurant (46) ($) *(1967 Calvert St. NW, 202-232-5431, www.mamaayeshas.com)* is a third-generation, family-owned institution serving Middle Eastern and Mediterranean food. Menu selections include Menzaleh, eggplant topped with ground beef, pine nuts, and tomato sauce. Or sample Mama's *mezzes*, including hummus (pureed chickpeas), baba ghanoush (roasted eggplant), and tabbouleh (ground wheat mixed with mint, parlsey, and lemon juice). For Ethiopian food, try **Meskerem (47) ($)** *(2434 18th St. NW, 202-462-4100)*, one of the best in DC. Dishes are meant to be shared and eaten with your fingers (no silverware here!) over basketlike tables. Live music

weekend evenings. The best choice for Brazilian cuisine is **The Grill from Ipanema (48) ($$-$$$)**  *(1858 Columbia Rd. NW, 202-986-0757, www.thegrilllfromipanema.com)*, serving authentic dishes, from seafood stews with palm oil and coconut milk to marinated grilled fish, seared steaks, and garlic chicken, accompanied by cocktails made with cachaça, a white liquor distilled from sugarcane. For comfort food, **Cashion's Eat Place (49) ($$)** *(1819 Columbia Rd. NW, 202-797-1819, www.cashions eatplace.com)* can't be beat. Black-and-white family photos line the walls, and seasonal Southern-style fare with French and Italian influences draws enthusiastic diners. Sample selections include seafood gumbo, Asian crispy whole fish, or a terrine of pork and veal. For flavorful regional Mexican cooking, including the best tamales in town, try **Mixtec (50) ($)** *(1792 Columbia Rd. NW, 202-332-1011)*, an informal café that's busy day and night. **Perry's (51) ($$)** *(1811 Columbia Rd. NW, 202-234-6218, www.perrysadamsmorgan.com)* pleases with American bistro and sushi selections and great views from its rooftop dining room. The Sunday "drag" brunch is an award-winner. For generous helpings of great-tasting pasta, **Pasta Mia (52) ($)** *(1790 Columbia Rd. NW, 202-328-9114)* is the place. But be prepared to wait.

Bars & Nightlife:

Felix/The Spy Lounge (53) *(2406 18th St. NW, 202-483-3549, www.thefelix.com)* opens at 5:00 PM and serves small plates of mini-burgers, spring rolls, and chicken satay meant for sharing. Their martinis, live music, and *Sex and the City* and *James Bond* videos draw crowds. Strut your stuff at **Habana Village (54)** *(1834 Columbia Rd. NW, 202-462-6310, www.habanavillage. com)*, offering Cuban cuisine, Latin music, and weekly salsa/meringue lessons. Mojitos anyone? For blues, R&B, jazz, and authentic soul food, don't miss **Madam's Organ (55)** *(2461 18th St. NW, 202-667-5370, www. madamsorgan.com)*, named one of the U.S.A.'s top bars by *Stuff* magazine. **Tryst Coffeehouse/Bar/Lounge (56)** *(2459 18th St. NW, 202-232-5500, www.trystdc.com)* is a fun, funky place to have a sandwich, sip a latte, or check your e-mail.

WHERE TO SHOP

Adams Morgan's international flavor translates into some of DC's most uncommon shopping experiences. For example, browse the multilevel brownstone that houses Skynear and Company (57) *(2122 18th St. NW, 202-797-7160, www.skynearonline. com)*. You'll find eclectic home furnishings from around the world. Shake Your Booty (58) *(2439 18th St. NW, 202-518-8205, www.shakeyourbootyshoes. com)* carries stylish shoes (and boots) for fashionistas on a budget. Fleet Feet Sports (59) *(1841 Columbia*

Rd. NW, 202-387-3888, www.fleetfeetdc.com) provides footwear and clothing for walkers, runners, and triathletes. For artsy finds, beads, and imported clothing, shop **Oya's Mini Bazaar (60)** (2420 18th St. NW, 202-667-9853). If you're looking for unique and inexpensive home furnishings from sofas to flatware, you'll find it at **Miss Pixie's Furnishings and Whatnot (61)** (2473 18th St. NW, 202-232-8171, www.misspixies.com).

WHERE TO STAY

Adam's Inn (62) ($) (1746 Lanier Pl. NW, 202-745-3600 or 800-578-6807, www.adamsinn.com), located in three 100-year-old Victorian buildings on a residential street, is a bed-and-breakfast known for its comfort, charm, and affordability. **Jurys Normandy Inn (63) ($-$$)** (2118 Wyoming Ave. NW, 202-483-1350, www.jurysdoyle.com) offers Old World charm and well-appointed rooms. Enjoy tea and cookies served in the parlor every afternoon. **American Guest House (64) ($-$$)** (2005 Columbia Rd. NW, 703-768-0335, www.americanguesthouse.com), an inn/B&B, is situated in a completely renovated 1889 home. Amenities include canopied beds, Wi-Fi Internet access, and full breakfast, including your choice of omelets and fresh fruit salad.

chapter 6

DUPONT CIRCLE/KALORAMA

U STREET/LOGAN CIRCLE

BROOKLAND

Places to See:

1. Dupont Memorial Fountain
2. Brewmaster's Castle
3. Patterson House
4. Woman's National Democratic Club
5. Anderson House
6. Townsend House
7. Spanish Steps
8. The Phillips Collection
9. Textile Museum
10. Woodrow Wilson House
11. Fondo del Sol Visual Arts Center
12. National Museum of American Jewish Military History
13. Burton Marinkovich Fine Art
14. Charles Sumner School Museum and Archives
15. Theater J
16. Alliance Française de Washington
39. Duke Ellington Mural
40. Spirit of Freedom Sculpture

41. African American Civil War Memorial Freedom Foundation and Museum
42. Thurgood Marshall Center for Service and Heritage
43. Mary McLeod Bethune Council House National Historic Site
44. Lincoln Theatre
45. Black Fashion Museum
46. HR-57: Center for the Preservation of Jazz and Blues
47. Studio Theatre
70. Catholic University of America
71. Trinity College
72. Basilica of the National Shrine of the Immaculate Conception
73. Pope John Paul II Cultural Center
74. Mount St. Sepulchre Franciscan Monastery
75. National Arboretum

Places to Eat & Drink:

17. Obelisk
18. Al Tiramisu
19. Lauriol Plaza
20. Kramerbooks & Afterwords Café & Grill
21. Komi
22. Pizzeria Paradiso
23. Firefly
24. The Big Hunt
25. Brickskeller
26. Topaz Bar
27. Fox and Hounds Lounge
48. Café Saint-Ex
49. Ben's Chili Bowl
50. Logan Tavern
51. P Street Bistro Café
52. Merkádo Kitchen
53. Gate 54
54. Black Cat
55. Helix Lounge
56. Bar Rouge

Where to Shop:

28. Top Shelf
29. Books-A-Million
30. Second Story Books
31. Beadazzled
32. Secondi
57. Pulp
58. Pop
59. Home Rule
60. Vastu
61. Muléh
62. Wild Women Wear Red
63. Good Wood
64. Habitat
65. Hemphill Fine Arts
66. Reincarnations

Where to Stay:

33. Hotel Madera
34. Topaz Hotel
35. Westin Embassy Row
36. Churchill Hotel
37. Hilton Washington
38. Hotel Tabard Inn
67. Hotel Rouge
68. Hotel Helix
69. DC GuestHouse

● *to Dupont Circle*

● SNAPSHOT ●

Dupont Circle is a cosmopolitan neighborhood that bustles with activity, drawing people of all types to its restaurants, bookstores, museums, embassies, coffee bars, and chess tables. The traffic circle itself is ideal for people-watching. Dupont Circle has grown from its Civil War–era rural roots, welcoming prominent people from throughout the city and the nation who built the mansions, many of which still line Massachusetts Avenue. These days, embassies, social clubs, private offices, think tanks, and other institutions fill the neighborhood's mansions. Today, Dupont Circle draws those seeking an international flavor, urban living, and diversity, including gays, lesbians, and bisexuals. Though primarily a residential neighborhood, Dupont Circle also offers some of the city's best museums and art galleries. Its northwestern boundaries defined by Rock Creek, Kalorama is an elegant private neighborhood that harbors five presidential homes.

PLACES TO SEE
Landmarks:

Start at the **Dupont Memorial Fountain (1)** *(Dupont Circle)*, named in honor of Samuel Francis Dupont, a Civil War naval hero. Three fluid figures representing the Arts of Ocean Navigation—the Sea, the Wind, and the Stars—decorate the base. Just south of the circle on Sunderland Place, you'll spot the wrought-iron fence of the **Brewmaster's Castle (2)** *(1307 New Hampshire Ave. NW, 202-429-1894, www.heurichhouse. org; walk-in tours two to three times daily)*. It's considered one of America's most intact late-Victorian homes, and an early "smart house"—with fireproofing, full plumbing, hot water, a central vac system, and more. The nearby **Patterson House (3)** *(15 Dupont Circle, 202-483-9200, www.thewashingtonclub.com)*, a Beaux-Arts mansion, was designed by Stanford White; it was the residence of the Calvin Coolidges in 1927 while the White House was undergoing repairs. Named for its original owner, Robert Patterson of Chicago, editor of the *Chicago Tribune*, and his wife, Elizabeth Medill Patterson, it was the setting for elaborate parties. Now called the Washington Club, it's home to a private social club. **Woman's National Democratic Club (4)** *(1526 New Hampshire Ave., 202-232-7363; www.democratic woman.org; tours by appointment; free admission)* has its home in the Whittemore House, named after opera singer Sarah Adams Whittemore, a descendant of President John Adams. The home exudes a fairy-tale look with its English slate roof, leaded glass windows, and turrets. Massachusetts Ave. west of Sheridan Circle is known as Embassy Row for the many embassies now housed in its stately mansions. Follow the circle around to Massachusetts Ave. heading northwest to the **Anderson House (5)** *(2118 Massachusetts Ave. NW, 202-785-2040; open Tues.–Sat. afternoons, www.thesociety ofthecincinnati.addr.com/anderson.htm)*, an Italianate palace built for career diplomat Larz Anderson III and his wife, Isabel Weld Perkins. Today it serves as headquarters for the Society of the Cincinnati, a benevolent organization established by George Washington for his officers and their direct descendants. It also has a collection of decorative and fine arts and Revolutionary War artifacts. The **Townsend House (6)** *(2121 Massachusetts Ave. NW, 202-387-7783, www.cosmos-club.org)* across the street was built in 1901 for railroad magnate Richard Townsend; it's now home to the Cosmos Club, a private club dedicated to the advancement of its members in science, literature, and art. Past Sheridan Circle, Massachusetts intersects with S Street. Turn right and continue east until you reach 22nd Street. Make another right, where you will see an unmarked dead end. Walk to the end to see Washington's version of Rome's **Spanish Steps (7)**; they once led to an 18th-century manor house called Kalorama, Greek for "beautiful view."

Arts & Entertainment:

The neighborhood boasts a variety of specialty museums, mostly situated north of the circle on R and S Streets. Don't miss **The Phillips Collection (8)** *(1600 21st St. NW, 202-387-2151, www.phillipscollection.org; free admission to the permanent collection; free Saturday walk-in tours, 2:00 PM, Thursday evening gallery talks at 6:00 PM and 7:00 PM, Sunday concerts, 5:00 PM October–May)*, the first modern art museum in the country. With nearly 2,500

works by American and European impressionists and modern artists, it is considered one of the world's finest small museums. It is home to Renoir's renowned *Luncheon of the Boating Party*, works by El Greco, van Gogh, Degas, Cézanne, Matisse, Monet, de Kooning, Hopper, and O'Keeffe. If textiles tickle your fancy, follow Massachusetts Ave. past Sheridan Circle to the **Textile Museum (9)** *(2320 S St. NW, 202-667-0441, www.textilemuseum.org)*, where 17,000 tapestries, carpets, clothing, and more, dating from 3,000 BC to the present, await. Learn through exhibits and a hands-on center that focuses on Oriental carpets and weavings from the Old World and New World, as well as pre-Columbian Peruvian and Islamic works. The **Woodrow Wilson House (10)** *(2340 S St. NW, 202-387-4062, www. woodrowwilsonhouse.org)* is the only presidential museum in the city. Wilson's final home after his

presidency, it depicts the 28th president's life and times through objects, furnishings, recordings, and silent films. **Fondo del Sol Visual Arts Center (11)** *(2112 R St. NW, 202-483-2777, www.dkmuseums.com/fondo.html)* devotes itself to the art, music, and culture of Latin, Caribbean, Native-American, and African-American peoples in Washington through exhibits, concerts, lectures, and poetry readings. Learn about the contributions of Jewish Americans in the U.S. Armed Services at the **National Museum of American Jewish Military History (12)** *(1811 R St. NW, 202-265-6280, Monday–Friday, 9:30 AM–5:00 PM, Sunday, 1:00 PM–5:00 PM, tours are available; archives access by appointment, www.nmajmh.org)*. You can view documents, medals, memorabilia, and firearms from American military  conflicts. Walking west, you'll discover a gem of an art gallery. **Burton Marinkovich Fine Art (13)** *(1506 21st St. NW, 202-296-6563, www.burtonmarinkovich.com)* displays prints, drawings, and paintings by modern and contemporary masters, such as Joan Miró and Alexander Calder. Learn more about local history at the **Charles Sumner School Museum and Archives (14)** *(1201 17th St. NW, 202-442-6060)*, site of the first public school for African-American students in Washington, and former headquarters for the superintendent and board of trustees for Colored Public Schools of Washington and Georgetown. East of Dupont Circle is progressive **Theater J (15)** *(Washington, DC Jewish Community Center, 1529 16th St. NW, 202-777-3229; box office,*

800-494-TIXZ or www.dcjcc.org/arts/theater); it's received numerous Helen Hayes Award nominations. For a range of courses, social activities, and cultural events pertaining to France, **Alliance Française de Washington (16)** *(2142 Wyoming Ave. NW, Monday–Friday, 10:00 AM to 6:00 PM, 202-234-7911, www. francedc.org)* is the place.

PLACES TO EAT & DRINK
Where to Eat:

Dupont Circle has more restaurants per block than almost any other Washington neighborhood. Here is a sampling of choices for cuisines in a variety of atmo-

spheres. For refined Italian, **Obelisk (17) ($$$)** *(2029 P St. NW, 202-872-1180)* serves divine five-course dinners, cheese course included. **Al Tiramisu (18) ($$-$$$)** *(2014 P St., 202-467-4466, www.altiramisu.com)*, another authentic Italian eatery, imports 90 percent of its ingredients, and all of its seafood and wine from Italy. You'll enjoy its friendly neighborhood feel. Lively atmosphere combines with moderately priced Mexican/Spanish food and refreshing margaritas at **Lauriol Plaza (19) ($)** *(1835 18th St. NW, 202-387-0035, www.lauriolplaza.com)*. Try *zarzuela de mariscos*, a seafood casserole of scallops, shrimp, fresh fish, squid, mussels, and clams, or *bistec a la criolla*, mesquite-grilled New York sirloin with sautéed Spanish onions. Don't miss **Kramerbooks & Afterwords Café & Grill (20) ($-$$)** *(1517 Connecticut Ave. NW,*

202-293-1002, www.kramers.com). A Washington institution since 1976, this American café and bookstore is perfect for a quick bite, coffee or cappuccino, or a full meal. Enjoy live music Wednesday through Saturday nights. Customer favorites include the bass, the crab cake  platter, spaghetti Bolognese, grilled filet mignon, or anything else grilled, including "today's catch." **Komi (21) ($$-$$$)** *(1509 17th St. NW, 202-332-9200)* is an oasis of casual tranquillity in this bustling neighborhood. Creative Greek-inspired dishes—grilled asparagus with watercress and feta, quail stuffed with foie gras and figs—are its forte. Known for the best pizza in town, **Pizzeria Paradiso (22) ($)** *(2029 P St. NW, 202-223-1245, www.eatyourpizza.com)*

serves up pies with crispy, chewy crust, baked in a wood-burning oven. A block and a half off Dupont Circle, you'll find **Firefly (23) ($-$$)** *(Hotel Madera, 1310 New Hampshire Ave. NW, 202-861-1310, www.firefly-dc.com)*, where tiny lanterns dangle from a faux tree and diners enjoy innovative American food, like double-cut pork chops with buttery potato puree or mushroom cassoulet with Oregon black truffles.

Bars & Nightlife:

The Big Hunt (24) *(1345 Connecticut Ave. NW, 202-785-2333, www.thebighunt.net)* draws regulars and newcomers to this laid-back, split-level bar. It features

Internet jukeboxes, pool tables, and a plethora of TV screens. Popular **Brickskeller (25)** *(1523 22nd St. O/P Sts. NW, 202-293-1885, www.the brickskeller.com)* is the place to go to sample a variety of beers. Located in a cellar, this cavelike pub features more than 1,000 brews from around the world. The **Topaz Bar (26)** *(1733 N St. NW, 202-393-3000)* features blue-velvet covered couches, leopard-patterned rugs, and changing colored lights that create an inviting atmosphere. Try their "Blue Nirvana"—champagne, vodka, and blue curaçao liqueur—and sample their Asian-inspired menu. **Fox and Hounds Lounge (27)** *(1537 17th St. NW, 202-232-6307)* has an eclectic clientele, and, patrons say, "the strongest mixed drinks in DC." Their large outdoor patio is perfect for hanging out and people-watching.

WHERE TO SHOP

Top Shelf (28) *(1627 Connecticut Ave. NW, 202-483-8050)* is a high-end purveyor of kitchen essentials, including loose and bagged tea, gadgets, espresso machines, teakettles, and French presses. Shelves of brand-new books abound at Books-A-Million (29) *(11 Dupont Cir., 202-319-1374, www.booksamillion.com)*, or browse the used and rare books, LP records, CDs, and DVDs at Second Story Books (30) *(2000 P St. NW, 202-659-8884, www.secondstorybooks.com)*. Beadazzled (31) *(150/ Connecticut Ave. NW, 202 265-2323, www.*

beadazzled.net) offers an amazing array of loose beads (glass, wood, shell, copper, silver, and gold); seed beads, pearl and gemstone beads, and art glass. They also sell all the tools and equipment you need to finish your bead projects. Secondi (32) *(1702 Connecticut Ave. NW, 2nd fl., 202-667-1122, www.secondi.com)* is a consignment shop that carries "good as new" designer fashions, including Chanel, Vuitton, Prada, and more.

WHERE TO STAY

For chic, contemporary accommodations, complete with coffeemakers with Starbucks coffee, animal-print robes, and Aveda bath products, you'll feel right at home at Hotel Madera (33) ($$) *(1310 New Hampshire Ave. NW, 202-296-7600 or 800-368-5691, www.hotel madera.com)*. It's just a block and a half from the circle itself. Cardio rooms—with treadmills or exercise bikes—and Nosh rooms with mini-kitchens are available on request. Serene surroundings, an in-room yoga channel, and morning power shakes await at the Topaz Hotel (34) ($$) *(1733 N St. NW, 202-393-3000 or 800-775-1202, www.topazhotel.com)*. The Westin Embassy Row (35) ($$$) *(2100 Massachusetts Ave. NW, 202-293-2100, www.westin.com)* boasts superb comfort, including custom beds and baths and a fitness center. Their complimentary "Love that Dog" program offers bowls, food, and beds for your four-legged companion. The hotel was the childhood home of Al Gore, when his father, the late Al Gore Sr.,

was a senator. Another option a little further from the heart of Dupont Circle is the **Churchill Hotel (36) ($-$$$)** *(1914 Connecticut Ave. NW, 202-797-2000 or 800-424-2464, www.thechurchillhotel.com)*, a Beaux-Arts gem, where historic elegance, spacious rooms, and modern amenities, like high-speed Internet access, mix. The legendary **Hilton Washington (37) ($$-$$$)** *(1919 Connecticut Ave. NW, 202-483-3000 or 800-HILTONS, www.washington.hilton.com)* is a huge 1,000-room-plus resort, offering landscaped gardens, an Olympic pool, and tennis courts. It's sometimes referred to as the "Reagan Hilton," because President Reagan was shot and wounded outside the hotel on March 30, 1981. The Victorian **Hotel Tabard Inn (38) ($-$$)** *(1739 N St. NW, 202-785-1277, www.tabardinn.com)* has 40 individually furnished sleeping rooms, some with private bath, some not. This popular historic inn does not have an elevator, though it does provide other modern comforts, including Wi-Fi Inernet access. Enjoy live jazz in the lounge on Sunday evenings.

● *to Mount Vernon Square/
7th Street-Convention Center, or U Street/African-
American Civil War Memorial/Cardozo*

● *to Farragut North*

●● *to McPherson Square*

● SNAPSHOT ●

Nearly destroyed after the riots that followed the assassination of Martin Luther King Jr., the U Street area, the soul of Washington's African-American community, has been revitalized and is now emerging as one of the most vibrant neighborhoods in the Capital City. U Street was home to jazz great Duke Ellington and poet Langston Hughes. "Black Broadway" nightclub-goers enjoyed performances by Pearl Bailey, Louis Armstrong, Cab Calloway, Lionel Hampton, Ella Fitzgerald, Billy Eckstine, Billie Holiday, and Sarah Vaughan, among others. Today, the neighborhood's historic Lincoln Theatre is home to jazz, comedy, poetry, and dance. With the opening of new clubs and restaurants, U Street and the adjacent area surrounding stately Logan Circle are drawing locals and visitors alike.

PLACES TO SEE
Landmarks:

One of the first things you'll see if you arrive by Metro at the U Street/African-American Civil War Memorial stop is the **Duke Ellington Mural (39)** *(1200 U St. NW, True Reformer Building)*, by G. Byron Peck; it's a 24-by 32-foot likeness of the jazz legend surveying the scene. The mural is an ever-present reminder of Ellington's impact on the neighborhood in its heyday during the first half of the 20th century. If you exit the Metro at Vermont Avenue, you'll see Ed Hamilton's **Spirit of Freedom Sculpture (40)** *(1000 U St. NW)* dedicated to black Civil War troops. Learn about their fight for freedom through photos and documents at the **African American Civil War Memorial Freedom Foundation and Museum (41)** *(1200 U St. NW, 202-667-2667, www.afroamcivilwar.org)*. Walking southwest to 12th Street, you'll pass the **Thurgood Marshall Center for Service and Heritage (42)** *(Twelfth Street/Anthony Bowen YMCA, 1816 12th St. T/S Sts. NW, 202-462-8314, www.thurgoodmarshallcenter.org)*, named for Thurgood Marshall, grandson of a slave, chief counsel for the NAACP, and Supreme Court Justice. Check out the museum on the first floor to learn more about the community and its famous residents, including Langston Hughes and Duke Ellington. Further south, Vermont Avenue, Rhode Island Avenue, and P Street intersect at Logan Circle. If you walk southwest on Vermont, you'll come across the **Mary McLeod Bethune Council House National Historic Site (43)** *(1318 Vermont Ave. NW, 202-673-2402, www.nps.gov/mamc)*. Bethune, a daughter of former slaves, was founder of the National Council of Negro Women and an advisor to four Presidents on African-American issues. This Victorian house was council headquarters and her home from 1943 to 1949. The

house is now a museum and home of the National Archives for Black Women's History.

Arts & Entertainment:

Near the Metro stop, you'll see the fabled **Lincoln Theatre (44)** *(1215 U St. 12th/13th Sts. NW, box office, 202-328-6000; tickets, 202-397-7328, www.thelincoln theatre.org)*, the 1920s venue that hosted myriad black music greats, now restored to its original glory. Public performances and private events, ranging from jazz concerts to poetry contests to school graduations take place here today. View African-American contributions to the fashion industry at the **Black Fashion Museum (45)** *(2007 Vermont Ave. NW, 202-667-0744, by appointment only, www.bfmdc.org)*. Walking southwest to 14th Street, you'll see **HR-57: Center for the Preservation of Jazz and Blues (46)** *(1610 14th St. NW, 202-667-3700, open Wed., Thurs. nights—jam sessions; Fri., Sat. nights—local/ national talent, www.hr57.org)*, a nonprofit musical cultural center that takes its name from the House resolution recognizing jazz as a rare and valuable national treasure. It offers lectures, workshops, lessons, concerts, and more. Artist-founded and artist-driven **Studio Theatre (47)** *(1501 14th St. NW, 202-332-3300,* *www.studiotheatre.org)* offers contemporary, edgy theater productions.

PLACES TO EAT & DRINK
Where to Eat:

The menu at **Café Saint-Ex (48) ($)** *(1847 14th St. NW, 202-265-7839, www.saint-ex.com)* includes sustainable organic and fresh local items when possible. Sample wild mushroom risotto or bistro-style seared mussels and a pint of specialty beer or ale. You'll enjoy the vin-

tage Art Deco aviation-themed decor. Follow in the footsteps of Duke Ellington, Miles Davis, Nat King Cole, Ella Fitzgerald, and Martin Luther King Jr. and experience authentic U Street at **Ben's Chili Bowl (49) ($)** *(1213 U St. NW, 202-667-0909, www.benschilibowl.com)*. Drawing crowds since 1958, Ben's is the place for classic chili con carne (or the vegetarian version), homemade potato salad, or cheese fries. Try the renowned chili half-smoke, Bill Cosby's favorite. For a laid-back bar-and-grill atmosphere with a local following, try **Logan Tavern (50) ($-$$)** *(1423 P St. NW, 202-332-3710, www.logantavern.com)* for choices like mixed greens and jicama salad, wasabi-crusted meat loaf, grilled tuna or salmon, and grilled turkey steak in maple and citrus. For a different twist on grilled food, try **P Street Bistro Café (51) ($)** *(1433 P St. NW, 202-234-6750)*. The ginger salmon and sweet potato fries are a departure from the usual. For a lovely "urban cantina" ambience and Latin-Asian cuisine, try **Merkádo Kitchen**

(52) ($$) *(1443 P St. NW, 202-299-0018, www. merkadodc.com)*. The menu includes coconut-crusted halibut, Baja California rolls, Asian paella, and Latin and Asian beers and sake.

Bars & Nightlife:

Gate 54 (53) *(1847 14th St. NW, 202-265-7839)* located downstairs in the **Café Saint-Ex (48)**, is a hip spot to have a drink and listen to some of the area's best DJs in an airplane hangar-inspired lounge. Rock out to alternative and independent live music at crowd-pleasing **Black Cat (54)** *(1811 14th St. NW, 202-667-7960, www.blackcatdc.com)*. You can also order a beer, a Texas veggie burger, listen to a poem, or just relax in the club's no-cover Red Room Bar, where you can play pinball or pool. Other nightspots are closer to Logan Circle and can be easily reached from the McPherson Square stop on the Blue or Orange Line. Just off Logan Circle, you'll find **Helix Lounge (55)** *(Helix Hotel, 1430 Rhode Island Ave. NW, 202-462-9001, www.helixlounge.com)* a cutting-edge hot spot where the lighting changes from moody blue to warm gold every few hours and patrons relax on ottoman-style chairs or converse on the outdoor patio. The club is famous for its Thursday Disco & Oreo nights, featuring '70s tunes and "Oreotinis." **Bar Rouge (56)** *(Hotel Rouge, 1315 16th St. NW, 202-232-8000, www.rougehotel.com)* with its upholstered walls, aluminum bar stools, and flat-screen video montage, is a red-hot hip place to relax and imbibe.

WHERE TO SHOP

U Street shoppers tend to favor the offbeat, the unique, and the unconventional. The U Street Metro stop on

the Green Line includes **Pulp (57)** *(1803 14th St. NW, 202-462-7857, www.pulpdc.com)*, the destination for out-of-the-ordinary greeting cards, gifts, and stationery. Up the stairs, you'll find hip clothing boutique **Pop (58)** *(1803A 14th St. NW, 202-332-3312, www.shoppop.com)*, featuring fashions from Free People, Penguin, and Ben Sherman, as well as new designers, plus funky jewelry and acces-

sories. **Home Rule (59)** *(1807 14th St. NW, 202-797-5544, www.homerule. com)* offers whimsical oven mitts, magnetic spice racks, illuminated ice cubes,

and kid-friendly flatware. For more home designs, stop at **Vastu (60)** *(1829 14th St. NW, 202-234-8344, www. vastudc.com)*, which takes its name from the Sanskrit belief that the arrangement of household objects promotes well-being. Browse its intriguing collection of custom-designed sofas, resin vases, and hardwood lamps. For home furnishings and fashions from Asia, **Muléh (61)** *(1831 14th St. NW, 202-667-3440, www.muleh.com)* is a must. Women who simply can't

own enough comfortable shoes should stop by **Wild Women Wear Red (62)** *(1512 U St. NW, 202-387-5700, www. wildwomenwearred.com)*, featuring comfortable, handmade footwear by Camper and Lisa Nading, among others. You can find jewelry and handbags, too. For 19th-century American antiques, decorative arts, pottery, and lamps visit Good Wood (63) *(1428 U St. NW, 202-986-3640, www.goodwooddc.com, closed Mon–Wed)*. You'll find more contemporary furniture and handcrafted jewelry at Habitat (64) *(1510 U St. NW, 202-518-7222, www.habitatstyle.com)*. Hemphill Fine Arts (65) *(1515 14th St. NW, 202-234-5601, www.hemphillfinearts.com)* shows the work of nationally recognized artists, as well as showcasing new, emerging artists. For an eclectic array of hand-painted household items, stop by Reincarnations (66) *(1401 14th St. NW, 202-319-1606, www.reincarnations.com)*.

WHERE TO STAY

Hotel Rouge (67) **($$)** *(1315 16th St. NW, 202-232-8000 or 800-368-5689, www.rougehotel.com)* is a deluxe boutique hotel in Scott Circle, three blocks from Logan Circle. Its creative guest rooms offer such amenities as 10-foot-long desks, flat-screen TVs, and red leather headboards. If you want to be closer to the U Street/Logan Circle action, stay at hip Hotel Helix (68) **($$)** *(1430 Rhode Island Ave. NW, 202-462-9001 or 800-706-1202, www.hotelhelix.com)*. Pop culture is the theme of this colorful hotel, with its platform beds, flat-screen TVs, and lime-green minibars. The DC GuestHouse

(69) ($$) *(1337 10th St. NW, 202-332-2502, www. dcguesthouse.com)*, a historic mansion one block from the convention center, features six spacious guest rooms decorated with beautiful art and rare furnishings from all over the world, and a handy business center. You'll enjoy the tasty, full breakfast and the relaxed, comfy furnishings.

● *to Brookland-CUA*

East of U Street is an outlying neighborhood called Brookland, situated around the Brookland/CUA Metro stop on the Red Line. Dubbed "Little Rome," it is home to the largest number of Catholic institutions (nearly 60) outside the Vatican. You'll find the **Catholic University of America (70)** *(620 Michigan Ave. NE, 202-319-5000, www.cua.edu)*, **Trinity College (71)** *(125 Michigan Ave. NE, 202-884-9000, www.trinitydc.edu)*, the **Basilica of the National Shrine of the Immaculate Conception (72)** *(400 Michigan Ave. NE, 202-526-8300, www.nationalshrine.com)*, which is the largest Catholic Church in the U.S.; the **Pope John Paul II Cultural Center (73)** *(3900 Harwood Rd. NE, 202-635-5400, www.jp2cc.org)*, and the **Mount St. Sepulchre Franciscan Monastery (74)**, *(1400 Quincy St. NE, 202-526-6800, www.myfranciscan.com)*, offering 40 acres of gardens, with replicas of famous gardens and shrines from the Holy Land. The African-American community also made this area home in the 1930s. Notable residents included Nobel Laureate Ralph Bunche and Pearl Bailey. The nearby **National Arboretum (75)** *(3501 New York Ave. NE, 202-245-2726, www.usna.usda.gov)*, a 444-acre sanctuary, features the National Bonsai and Penjing Museum, and the National Herb Garden.

chapter 7

SOUTHWEST WATERFRONT

ANACOSTIA

5th St

stia
k

SOUTHWEST WATERFRONT
ANACOSTIA

Places to See:
1. *Titanic* Memorial
2. Fort Lesley J. McNair
3. Thomas Law House
4. Wheat Row
5. St. Dominic's Church
6. Benjamin Banneker Park
7. Odyssey
8. Spirit Cruises
9. Arena Stage
10. Washington Navy Yard
26. Frederick Douglass National Historic Site
27. Fort Stanton and Washington Overlook
28. Fort Dupont Park
29. Anacostia Museum
30. Anacostia Park
31. Kenilworth Park and Aquatic Gardens

Places to Eat & Drink:
11. CityZen
12. Café MoZU
13. Phillips Flagship
14. Pier 7
15. Cantina Marina
16. Market Inn Restaurant
17. H2O Restaurant and Lounge
18. Zanzibar on the Waterfront
19. Empress Lounge

Where to Shop:
20. Maine Avenue Fish Wharf

Where to Stay:
21. Channel Inn
22. L'Enfant Plaza Hotel
23. Mandarin Oriental Hotel
24. Residence Inn Marriott Washington, DC/Capitol
25. Best Western Capitol Skyline Hotel

●●●● *to L'Enfant Plaza*

●● *to Federal Center SW*

● *to Waterfront-SEU, or Navy Yard*

● SNAPSHOT ●

Just south of the Washington Mall you'll find **L'Enfant Plaza**, where a new state-of-the-art children's museum is scheduled to open in 2009. Further south is the neighborhood known as Southwest Waterfront. A former working-class, immigrant neighborhood revitalized in the fifties, the area was part of the Underground Railroad, and home of Al Jolson. One of its chief landmarks is Arena Stage, established in 1950, now a three-theater complex, including a Tony Award-winning resident theater. One of the attractions of the Southwest Waterfront neighborhood is, naturally, its proximity to the water. The Washington Channel—between East Potomac Park and the neighborhood itself—is filled with sailboats, yachts, fishing boats, and cruise tour boats. Though Capitol Hill is close at hand, it seems far away from this self-contained, waterfront neighborhood.

PLACES TO SEE
Landmarks:

Most of the buildings in this area house federal agencies, such as the Federal Aviation Administration, the Department of Education, the Department of Agriculture, and the Department of Health and Human Services; these are not open to tourists. To reach the waterfront, take the Green Line to Waterfront/SEU. At the end of the promenade near the **Washington Channel** is a small park that serves as the backdrop for the ***Titanic Memorial (1)*** *(4th and P Sts. SW)*, a sculpture dedicated to the men who died in the *Titanic* shipwreck in 1912 trying to save the lives of women and children. Further south along the channel is **Fort Lesley J. McNair (2)** *(4th and P Sts. SW, 703-545-6700)*. More than two centuries old, it was built to defend the capital city at Greenleaf Point, where the Potomac River and the Anacostia meet. This was also the site where Lincoln assassination conspirators were tried and hanged.

The **Thomas Law House (3)** *(1252 6th St. SW)*, built in 1796, is a three-story Federal-style house, first occupied by Thomas Law and his wife, Elizabeth Custis, a granddaughter of Martha Washington. Renovated in 1965, it now serves as the community center for Tiber  Island residents. Although it is not open to the public, it can be rented out for special events. Nearby historic **Wheat Row (4)** *(1315-21 4th St. SW)* built in 1795, are probably the earliest row houses built in DC. Walking north, you'll see **St. Dominic's Church (5)** *(630 E St. SW, 202-554-7863, www.st-dominic-church.org)*, a Gothic landmark dating from 1875, known for its stained-glass windows and 250-foot steeple. **Benjamin Banneker Park (6)** *(10th and G Sts. SW)* memorializes the scientist hired by George Washington to assist in the surveying of the area that would become the District of Columbia.

Arts & Entertainment:

For an experience that will appeal to all of your senses, sail on the **Odyssey (7)** *(Gangplank Marina, 600 Water St. SW, 888-741-0281 or 202-488-6030, www.odysseycruises.com)* where you will cruise on the Potomac River, eat a sumptuous meal, and listen and dance to live music. Another dining/dancing cruise line is **Spirit Cruises (8)** *(Pier 4, 6th and Water Sts. SW, 202-554-8013 or 866-211-3811, www.spiritcruises.com)*. Sail on their *Spirit of Washington II*, which will take you to Mount Vernon, George Washington's home. Easily accessible from the Waterfront/SEU Metro stop, award-winning **Arena Stage (9)** *(1101 6th St. SW, 202-488-3300, www.arenastage.org)* DC's largest non-profit theater, produces classic American dramas, comedies, and musicals, as well as new plays and works in progress. For a change of pace, take the Metro to the **Washington Navy Yard (10)** *(9th and M Sts.)*. This area served as the Naval gun factory during the 19th century. Visit the **Navy Museum** *(805 Kidder Breese SE, call in*

advance for an appointment, 202-433-4882, www.history.navy.mil). It spans more than 200 years of naval history, including showcasing weapons and battles, from the Revolutionary War through Desert Storm. Next door to the Navy Museum is the **USS *Barry***, a Cold War-era destroyer ship that you can tour. The **Marine Corps Museum**, *(901 M St. SE, 202-433-3840)* displays flags, trophies, and personal effects of some of their members.

PLACES TO EAT & DRINK
Where to Eat:

Named one of the "Hottest Restaurants in the World" by *Food & Wine*, **CityZen (11) ($$$)** *(Mandarin Oriental Hotel, 1330 Maryland Ave. SW, 202-787-6006, www.mandarinoriental.com/washington)* provides the perfect special-occasion dining experience. The sleek decor artfully combines the elements of wood, water, fire, earth, and metal. Enjoy a drink as you watch the activity in the exhibition kitchen. CityZen also boasts an impressive single malt whiskey collection, an array of rare cognacs, and a wine cellar with over 800 selections. For contemporary cuisine with an Asian flair and Potomac views, choose **Café MoZU (12) ($$$)** *(Mandarin Oriental Hotel, 1330 Maryland Ave. SW, 202-767-6868, www.mandarinoriental.com/washington)*, also found in the Mandarin Oriental Hotel. **Phillips Flagship (13) ($$)** *(900 Water St. SW, 202-488-8515, www.phillipsseafood.com/phillipsflagship)* is known for its bountiful all-you-can-eat seafood buffet, sushi bar, or a traditional menu, as you enjoy the water view. Great seafood and views can be found at **Pier 7 (14) ($$)** *(650 Water St. SW,*

202-554-2500, www.channelinn.com), the oldest family-owned and operated restaurant on the waterfront. For casual Cajun fare, flip-flop-and-shorts ambience, live music, and fun happy hours, choose **Cantina Marina (15) ($)** *(600 Water St. SW, 202-554-8396, www. cantinamarina.com)*, located right on the dock.

Bars & Nightlife:

The **Market Inn Restaurant (16)** *(200 E. St. SW, 202-554-2100, www.marketinnrestaurant.com)*, near the Federal Center SW Metro stop and Smithsonian museums has been a Southwest landmark since 1959. Their menu offers more than 85 seafood and beef entrées. You can even select your own lobster from the tank! Enjoy live piano and jazz music. A champagne jazz buffet brunch is offered on Sundays. Trendy **H2O Restaurant and Lounge (17)** *(800 Water St. SW, 202-484-6300, www. h2odc.com)* offers stunning waterfront views, happy hour, live entertainment, guest celebrities, and a menu that features seafood and American cuisine. **Zanzibar on the Waterfront (18)** *(700 Water St. SW, 202-554-9100)* serves authentic Caribbean food, and after the kitchen closes, it's a dance club with a DJ, and live jazz, blues, and Latin-inspired music. Enjoy a signature martini at the **Empress Lounge (19)** *(Mandarin Oriental Hotel, 1330 Maryland Ave. SW, 202-787-6006, wwww.mandarinoriental.com/Washington)* as you watch the upscale crowd. Listen to piano music and jazz on weekend evenings.

WHERE TO SHOP

On the northern end of the promenade, the Maine Avenue Fish Wharf (20) *(1100 Maine Ave. SW)*, also known as The Wharf, is an open-air fish market where you can enjoy a taste of the old Southwest waterfront. Locals barter for fish, crabs, and lobsters sold from floating barges. These barges are reminiscent of the original system when fishing boats would journey back and forth from Colonial Beach, Virginia, after harvesting the bay.

WHERE TO STAY

Check out Channel Inn (21) (\$\$) *(650 Water St. 202-554-2400 or 800-368-5668, www.channelinn.com)*, DC's only waterfront hotel located on a channel of the Potomac River. Comfortable, charmingly decorated rooms all have balconies. Providing well-appointed accommodations, a rooftop pool, a restaurant, lounge, and pub, L'Enfant Plaza Hotel (22) (\$\$-\$\$\$) *(480 L'Enfant Plaza SW, 202-484-1000 or 800-635-5065, www.lenfantplazahotel.com)*, is steps away from the L'Enfant Plaza Metro stop, and a short walk to the Smithsonian museums. For luxury, sophistication, and exceptional dining, choose the Mandarin Oriental Hotel (23) (\$\$\$) *(1330 Maryland Ave. SW, 202-554-8588 or 888-888-1778, www.mandarinoriental.com/washington)*. Enjoy the feng-shui-influenced rooms, state-of-the-art fitness center, heated lap pool, and views. Residence Inn Marriott Washington, DC/ Capitol (24) (\$\$) *(333 E. St. SW,*

202-484-8280 or 800-331-3131, www.capitolmarriott. com) is an all-suite hotel, complete with fully outfitted kitchens and complimentary hot breakfast buffet. It's the perfect "home away from home." For good value try the **Best Western Capitol Skyline Hotel (25) ($-$$)** *(101 I St. SW, 202-488-7500 or 800-458-7500, www. bestwestern.com)* offering newly renovated rooms, a competition-sized swimming pool, and complimentary shuttle service to key sites and Metro stops.

ANACOSTIA

● *to Anacostia*

● *to Deanwood*

● SNAPSHOT ●

Anacostia, the district east of the Anacostia River, was one of the first planned suburbs of DC. Reach the neighborhood via Metro's Green Line to the Anacostia stop or drive across the 11th Street Bridge. There are several historic and natural gems in this area, but visitors should take care because it does have a high crime rate. Anacostia is the home of Cedar Hill, the beautifully preserved home of Frederick Douglass, former slave, diplomat, publisher, and presidential advisor. It's also the home of the Smithsonian's Anacostia Museum and Center for African-American History and Culture. Kenilworth Park and Aquatic Gardens is an unexpected oasis filled with lotuses and water lilies. A brand-new baseball stadium is undergoing construction now, and should be open for the 2008 season. At the present, there are no hotels or shops to speak of; however, a major revitalization of the area is planned.

PLACES TO SEE
Landmarks:

Take the B2 Metro bus from the Anacostia Metro stop to the **Frederick Douglass National Historic Site (26)** *(1411 W*

St. SE, 202-426-5961 or 800-967-2283, www.nps.gov/frdo). The American abolitionist moved to this handsome Victorian home in 1877; he lived here until his death in 1895. The home, named "Cedar Hill" by Douglass, offers a unique glimpse into the past. Many of Douglass's personal possessions remain here: his bowler hat and eyeglasses; a cane owned by Abraham Lincoln (and given to Douglass by Mary Todd Lincoln); and his personal 1,200 volume library. The Visitor Center offers a 17-minute film about the abolitionist. Ranger-led tours offer more information; reservations are encouraged. For a spectacular view of the city, take the Anacostia Metro or W1 or W2 Metro bus toward Naylor and Good Hope Roads, to **Fort Stanton and Washington Overlook (27)** *(Erie Street near Morris Road; parking lot of Our Lady of Perpetual Help Catholic Church).* The fort site is in the woods adjacent to the parking lot; an historic marker stands in the corner of the lot. Situated 380 feet above the Potomac River, this overlook stands adjacent to the original site of Fort Stanton, dating to 1861 as the first of some 60 forts that surrounded the city to protect it from Confederate attacks during the Civil War. Another fort that defended the southern border of the city is **Fort Dupont Park (28)** *(Randall Circle SE and Minnesota Ave., 202-426-5961, www.nps.gov/fodu),* 376 acres of densely wooded parkland dotted with trails, tennis and basketball courts, and softball fields. In addition, there is an ice rink and a National Park Service-staffed Community Nature Center, and Civil War programs. During summer evenings on weekends, free jazz concerts are held in the outdoor theater.

Arts & Entertainment:

The **Anacostia Museum (29)** *(1901 Fort Pl. SE, 202-633-4870, www.anacostia.si.edu)*, a branch of the Smithsonian, features a collection of changing exhibits on African-American art, history, and culture. **Anacostia Park (30)** *(entrance to Kenilworth Park recreation area at the westernmost end of Nannie Helen Burroughs Avenue NE, just off I-295 or Kenilworth Avenue, www. nps.gov/nace/anacostia.htm)* covers more than 1,200 acres in Anacostia along the Anacostia River. If you're looking to spot wildlife or play golf—there's the 18-hole Langston Golf Course and a driving range—tennis, or basketball, this is the place. Looking for something different? Head to the roller-skating rink or bring the family for a picnic or boating in the Anacostia. **Kenilworth Park and Aquatic Gardens (31)** *(northeastern section of Anacostia Park, Anacostia Avenue and Douglas St. NE, 202-426-6905, www.nps.gov/nace/kepa; 30-minute tours available, free. Take Metro's Orange Line to the Deanwood stop, exit toward Polk Street, walk a block over the I-295 overpass, follow Douglas Street two blocks, then follow park signs)* is a little-known natural haven that constitutes about 700 acres and is part of Anacostia Park. It's the only National Park Service site dedicated to showcasing and growing aquatic plants. The Gardens began as a hobby for Civil War veteran W. B. Shaw in 1882. His daughter, L. Helen Fowler, continued his efforts until the Gardens were purchased by the government in 1938. If you walk the River Trail, located on the northern edge of the marsh, you may be able to spot some local wildlife and birds. Early morning is the best time to visit.

chapter 8

VIRGINIA SUBURBS—
ALEXANDRIA, ARLINGTON,
AND BEYOND

MARYLAND SUBURBS—
BETHESDA AND BEYOND

Places to See:

1. Alexandria
2. Arlington
3. McLean/Great Falls Park
4. Mount Vernon
5. Bethesda
6. Chevy Chase/Audubon
   Naturalist Society
7. Glen Echo/Glen Echo Park
8. Potomac/C&O Canal
   National Historic Park
9. Wheaton/Brookside
   Gardens

Note: This map only contains bullets for the town or city where the site is located.

It is sometimes called the City of Magnificent Distances, but it might with greater propriety be termed the City of Magnificent Intentions…

—*Charles Dickens*

● SNAPSHOT ●

The Virginia suburbs of Washington, DC, include a diverse and historic collection of destinations within easy access to downtown DC. Whether you drive or rely on public transportation, you can reach most major landmarks, arts and entertainment spots, eateries, shopping, and hotels in the suburbs within 30 minutes. This section focuses on key places nearby, in Arlington County, Alexandria, and Fairfax County. Arlington is home to a number of important sights, including Arlington National Cemetery and the Marine Corps War Memorial sculpture of the famous photo of the 1945 flag-raising on Iwo Jima. Old Town Alexandria (King Street Metro stops, Blue or Yellow Line) offers antiquing, shopping, historic homes, and more. Is your time limited? Then the must-do site is George Washington's home at Mount Vernon in Fairfax County.

⚫⚪ *to King Street,*
or Pentagon City, or Pentagon

PLACES TO SEE
Landmarks:

Take the King Street Metro stop on the Blue or Yellow Line to reach the heart of Old Town Alexandria, a revitalized colonial town. The two main arteries here are Washington Street, running north and south, and King Street, running east and west, part of a grid that stretches to the Potomac River on the east and to the Braddock Road Metro stop on the northwest. From King Street Metro, walk east along King Street, cross Washington Street, and continue east. Old Town Alexandria is a gem of a place, where history meets the waterfront, where Scottish roots and small-town, Southern hospitality combine. Wander its cobblestone streets; you'll love its art galleries, gourmet restaurants, home furnishings, antiques shops, and museums. Start at King Street and turn right on South Washington Street; here you'll find some of the Old Town's most appealing historic places. Stop first at **The Lyceum** *(201 S. Washington St., corner of Prince St., 703-838-4994, www.alexandriahistory.org).*

175

Housed in a superb two-story 1839 Greek Revival structure, it presents the city's history through documents, photographs, furniture, decorative arts, tools, and Civil War artifacts. Return to King Street and walk east toward the river to **Gadsby's Tavern Museum** *(134 N. Royal St., 703-838-4242, www.gadsbystavern.org)*. George Washington and Thomas Jefferson, among other early American notables, were guests at this restored 18th-century hotel and tavern. **Market Square** *(301 King St.)* is home of the nation's oldest, continuously operating same-site Farmers' Market *(301 King St., Saturdays from 5 AM to 10 AM)*, offering fresh veggies, fruits, honey, baked goods, plants, quilts, and more. **Carlyle House** *(121 N. Fairfax St., 703-549-2997, www.carlylehouse.org)*, a block away, is a Georgian Palladian manor household dating to 1753, built by city founder John Carlyle, a Scottish merchant. This was where General Edward Braddock planned strategies of the French and Indian War in 1775. If you need help with your stay in Alexandria, stop at **Ramsay House**, Alexandria's oldest house and its modern-day visitors center *(221 King St., 703-838-4200 or 800-388-9119, www.funside.com)*. Another historic place is the **Stabler-Leadbeater Apothecary Museum** *(105–107 S. Fairfax St., 703-836-3713, www.apothecarymuseum.org)*.  Quaker Edward Stabler began his family pharmacy here in 1792. Most of the furnishings, herbs, and potions remain intact. Famous patrons included George and Martha Washington and Robert E. Lee.

Arts & Entertainment:

At the foot of King Street in Alexandria is the **Torpedo Factory Art Center** *(105 N. Union St., 703-838-4565, www.torpedofactory.org; open daily, 10 AM to 5 PM)*. This former U.S. Navy torpedo plant houses the studios and workshops of over 160 painters, potters, sculptors, and other artisans. Most of the arts and crafts are for sale. It's also home to the **Art League School** and the **Alexandria Archaeology Museum** *(www.alexandriaarchaeology.org)*. The **Little Theatre of Alexandria** *(600 Wolfe St., 703-683-0496, www.thelittletheatre.com)* the oldest award-winning community theater group in the DC area, boasts a seven-show season. The **Old Town Theater** *(815-1/2 King St., 703-683-8888, http://tickets.oldtowntheater.com)*, built in 1914, showcases all sorts of performing arts, including movies, music, and children's shows. The **Birchmere Music Hall** *(3701 Mount Vernon Ave., 703-549-7500, www.birchmere.com)* draws crowds with concerts featuring top names in country, folk, blues, and alternative music.

PLACES TO EAT AND DRINK

Eateries of every kind line the streets of Old Town Alexandria *(King Street Metro stop, Blue or Yellow Line)*. At the foot of King Street near the water, you'll find **The Fish Market ($-$$)** *(105 King St., 703-836-5676, www.fishmarketoldtown.com)*, located in a 200-year-old historic building, and known for its clam chowder, oysters, crab cakes, and lively atmosphere. Nearby is the **Chart House ($$-$$$)** *(One Cameron St., 703-684-5080, www.chart-house.com)*, part of a national chain. It offers seafood, steak, and great views of the Potomac River. Signature dishes include snapper Hemingway and hot chocolate lava cake. On summer evenings head to **The Scoop Grill & Homemade Ice Cream ($)** *(110 King St., 703-549-4527)* for frozen custard, yogurt, and homemade ice cream in a fifties-style setting. Another choice for sweets is **Ben & Jerry's Alexandria Scoop Shop ($)** *(103 S. Union St., 703-684-8866, www.benjerry.com)*, an "oasis of ice cream euphoria." Just a few doors down, the inviting **Union Street Public House ($$)** *(121 S. Union St., 703-548-1785, www.usphalexandria.com)* treats you to Southern regional American specialties in an Old World tavern-style ambience. Prefer Italian? **Landini Brothers ($$-$$$)** *(115 King St., 703-836-8404, www. landinibrothers.com)* stone and mahogany dining room is the perfect place for traditional Tuscan fare. And you'll find over 150 choices on the wine list. **The Wharf ($-$$$)** *(119 King St., 703-836-2836, www.wharfrestaurant. com)* features 1790s architecture, including charred beams from the Civil War, and combines seasonal Chesapeake favorites with contemporary dishes. **Il Porto Ristorante ($$)** *(121 King St., at the corner of Lee Street, 703-836-8833, www.ilportoristorante.com)* serves fine Italian cuisine in this cozy, dimly lit dining room in the heart of Old Town Alexandria. Enjoy steak and seafood in casual yet elegant environs at **The Warehouse Bar & Grill ($$)** *(214 King St., 703-683-6868, www. warehousebarandgrill.com)*. The decor of this historic building features caricatures of the local gentry. Have a drink at the antique mahogany bar. At the other end of King Street, closer to the Metro, is **Las Tapas Restaurant**

($-$$$) *(710 King St., 703-836-4000, www.lastapas.us)* featuring over 62 varieties of tapas, wines, and sherries from Spain, along with flamenco dancers and Spanish guitar music. The sophisticated **Morrison House Grille ($$-$$$)** *(Morrison House Hotel, 116 S. Alfred St., 703-838-8000 or 866-834-6628, www.morrisonhouse.com)* is the place for wild game fish, free-range fowl, fine meat, fresh produce, and first-rate service. The warm and friendly **Taverna Cretekou ($-$$)** *(818 King St., 703-548-8688, www.tavernacretekou.com)* serves authentic Mediterranean specialties in a setting reminiscent of the

Greek Isles. For Texas, Cincinnati, or vegetarian chili, try the original **Hard Times Café ($)** *(1404 King St., 703-837-0050, www.hardtimes.com)*, and enjoy the country-western jukebox with your beer. One of the most romantic restaurants in the area is located north of Old Town on the Potomac River. **Indigo Landing ($$)** *(Washington Sailing Marina, George Washington Pky., 703-548-0001, www.indigolanding.com)* offers contemporary, low-country cuisine in a setting overlooking the Washington Sailing Marina. Try the white grit bisque with lobster-porkcheek dumplings and cornbread dust. For dessert, have a fresh doughnut rolled in coconut, with caramel sauce for dipping.

WHERE TO SHOP

Can't resist decorative arts, antiques, clothing boutiques, and gift emporiums? Old Town Alexandria *(King Street*

Metro stop, Blue or Yellow Line) is for you. Toward the foot of King Street, you'll find **The Winterthur Museum Store** *(207 King St., 703-684-6092, www.winterthur. org)*, which carries decorative items related to Winterthur, the Henry Francis du Pont estate in Winterthur, Delaware. Nearby is **The Virginia Shop** *(104*

S. Union St., 703-836-3160 or 888-297-8288, www.thevirginiashop.com), a cornucopia of traditional decorative arts and accessories, Virginia wines, fudge, peanuts, biscuit mixes, and other souvenirs displayed in a 1765 historic two-story structure. Experience real Southern hospitality while you shop. **Why Not?** is a fun place to shop, with or without kids, *(200 King St., 703-548-4420)* and revisit childhood through its toys, books, games, and clothes. If you can't get enough of Christmas ornaments, Halloween ghosts, or Thanksgiving turkeys, head around the corner to **The Christmas Attic** *(125 Union St., 703-548-2829 or 800-881-0084, www.christmasattic.com)*. Closer to the King Street Metro stop, bargain hunters will love the **Crate and Barrel Outlet** *(1700 Prince St., 703-739-8800, www.crateandbarrel.com)*, the place to find home designs discounted up to 70 percent. If you're looking for sweets, stop at **Kingsbury Chocolates** *(1017 King St., 2nd fl., 703-548-2800, www.kingsburychocolates.com)* for unique confections like chipotle-cinnamon truffles, lavender-pistachio hot chocolate, and Turkish apricots dipped in dark chocolate. **HazelSnooks** *(111 S. Alfred St., 703-683-8343, www.hazelsnooks.com)* stocks fudge, brittle, cookies, brownies, and sweet and spicy nuts. Many of their wares are made from family recipes. **Tradition de France** *(1113 King St., 703-836-5340, www.traditiondefrance.com)* features three floors of hand-made imported French furniture, including armoires, leather couches, and tables with inlaid patterns and marble inserts. For an eclectic assortment of antique and new furniture and accessories, visit **Random Harvest** *(810 King St., 703-548-8820, www.randomharvesthome.com)*.

WHERE TO STAY

If you prefer colonial elegance, stay at the Old Town's **Morrison House ($$$)** *(116 S. Alfred St., 703-838-8000 or 866-834-6628, www.morrisonhouse.com)*, an 18th-century–style inn with four-poster beds, intimate public rooms, decorative fireplaces, and an acclaimed restaurant. It's ten blocks from the King Street Metro. The only hotel in the historic district, the **Holiday Inn Select Old Town ($$-$$$)** *(480 King St., 703-549-6080 or 800-HOLIDAY, www.hiselect.com/axe-oldtown)* is rated one of the top 75 Holiday Inns internationally, and offers a large indoor pool and a fitness center. For good value and a welcoming atmosphere on the north end of Old Town, stay at the **Best Western Old Colony Inn ($-$$)** *(1101 N. Washington St., 703-739-2222 or 800-528-1234, www.hotel-alexandria.com)*. A hot breakfast buffet comes with your room, and the hotel offers a free shuttle service to the center of Old Town, a business center, a fitness center, and high-speed Internet access.

ARLINGTON (2), VIRGINIA

●● *to Rosslyn*

● *to Arlington Cemetery*

●● *to Pentagon, or Pentagon City*

● *to Clarendon, or Ballston-MU*

PLACES TO SEE
Landmarks:

To organize your visit, find brochures, bus schedules, exhibits, and watch a multimedia production, stop at the **Arlington Visitors Center** *(1301 S. Joyce St., 800-677-6267, Pentagon City Metro stop, Blue or Yellow Line)*. You can then walk to the **Marine Corps War Memorial**, commonly known as the **Iwo Jima Memorial**, *(exit the Metro, turn right on Moore Street, go to end of block turn left, go 1/2 block to Lynn Street, cross Lynn and turn right, follow the sidewalk along the Route 50 overpass to the memorial on the left,*

703-289-2500, www.nps.gov/gwmp/usmc.htm). The largest cast bronze statue in the world, it re-creates the raising of the American flag on Mount Suribachi during World War II, and is dedicated to all Marines who have died in battle since 1775. From the surrounding park you'll enjoy breathtaking views of the Washington Monument, the Lincoln Memorial, and the Capitol. If you're in Washington for Independence Day, it's an ideal place from which to watch the fireworks display. Within the same park is the 127-foot-tall **Netherlands Carillon** *(next to the Iwo Jima Memorial, 703-289-2500, www.nps.gov/gwmp/carillon.htm)*, a 50-bell tower the Dutch people gave to the U.S. in gratitude for its aid during and after World War II. The carillon plays "Westminster Chimes" each hour and Armed Forces anthems, U.S. and Netherlands anthems, and other selections at noon and 6 PM. The park service Web site lists the full program schedule. From the Arlington Cemetery Metro stop on the Blue Line, visit **Arlington National Cemetery** *(Memorial Dr. and Jefferson Davis Hwy., 703-607-8000, www.arlingtoncemetery.org/index.htm)*, a national shrine to over a quarter of a million men and women who have died defending the U.S., from Revolutionary soldiers to Operation Iraqi Freedom, as well as veterans and former slaves. The cemetery's **Visitor Center** is located about a block from the cemetery, where you can obtain tickets for the **"Tourmobile"** *(202-554-5100, www.tourmobile.com)*, which will drive you through the cemetery. You'll want to see the Tomb of the Unknowns, where soldiers from World Wars I and II and the Korean War are buried. Time your visit to see the changing of the guard in front of these tombs. John F. Kennedy is buried here, along with his wife,

Jacqueline, and his brother Robert. Kennedy's grave is marked with an "Eternal Flame." The grounds of **Arlington House/The Robert E. Lee Memorial** *(Arlington*  *National Cemetery, 703-235-1530, www.nps.gov/arho)* offer spectacular views of DC. This is the former home of George Washington's adopted grandson, George Washington Parke Custis, whose daughter, Mary Anna Randolph, married Robert E. Lee. It was here that Lee resigned his commission in the U.S. Army to fight for the South. The federal government confiscated the property and designated a 200-acre section as a military cemetery. To the southeast, **The Pentagon**, spread over 34 acres *(the Pentagon Metro stop on the Blue or Yellow Line; tours available for groups, educational organizations, and active military personnel by two-week advance reservation only; 703-697-1776, http://pentagon.afis.osd.mil/tours.cfm)* is headquarters of the Department of Defense. It's one of the world's largest office buildings (three times the floor space of the Empire State Building), with over 17 miles of corridor, yet it takes only seven minutes to walk between any two points in the building.

Arts & Entertainment:

Take the Metro to Pentagon City on the Blue or Yellow Line to the **Drug Enforcement Administration Museum and Visitors Center** *(700 Army Navy Dr., Pentagon City, 202-307-3463; reservations required for groups of 15 or more, www.deamuseum.org)*; here you'll learn how the illicit drug industry has affected American society and how federal law enforcement tries to control these substances through "Illegal Drugs in America: A Modern History," the permanent exhibition.

PLACES TO EAT & DRINK

For that classic American chili parlor experience, it's hard to beat the **Hard Times Café ($)** *(3028 Wilson Blvd., 703-528-2233, Clarendon Metro stop, Orange Line, www.hardtimes.com)*. Try its "Chili Bubba," cornbread topped with chili, cheddar cheese, tomatoes, onions, and sour cream. **Little Viet Garden ($$)** *(3012 Wilson Blvd., 703-522-9686, Clarendon Metro stop, Orange Line)* draws crowds with its Asian offerings and large outdoor terrace. Prefer Tex-Mex? Choose **Uncle Julio's Rio Grande Café ($-$$)** *(4301 N. Fairfax Drive, 703-528-3131, www.unclejulios.com, Ballston/MU Metro stop, Orange Line)* for fajitas, margaritas, and a festive atmosphere. For Memphis barbecue and rhythm and blues, try **Red Hot & Blue BBQ ($)** *(1600 Wilson Blvd., 703-276-7427, Rosslyn Metro stop, Blue or Orange Line, www.redhotandblue.com)*, serving plentiful portions with friendly Southern style. **Tom Sarris' Orleans House ($-$$)** *(1213 Wilson Blvd., 703-524-2929, Rosslyn Metro stop, Blue or Orange Line)* is known for its prime rib, seafood, and a salad bar that spills over with selections. For creative American fare in relaxed surroundings, choose **Bistro Bistro ($-$$)** *(4021 S. 28th St., 703-379-0300,* *www.bistro-bistro.com, The Village at Shirlington, off I-395).*

WHERE TO SHOP

The Fashion Centre at Pentagon City *(1100 S. Hayes St., 703-415-2400, www.simon.com, Pentagon City Metro stop, Blue or Yellow Line)* ranks as one of the most popular in the Washington, DC region. Convenient to downtown, it draws crowds to its 170 stores, a food court, full-service restaurants, and the Ritz-Carlton Hotel. A glass-enclosed, sky-lit, multilevel shopping

 adventure, its stores range from Macy's and Nordstrom to stylish specialty shops, such as Crabtree & Evelyn, Sephora, and Godiva Chocolatier. Nearby **Pentagon Row** *(1101 S. Joyce St., 703-413-6690, www.pentagonrow.com, Pentagon City Metro stop, Blue or Yellow Line)* features specialty retailers, cafés, a gym, Starbucks, an Irish pub, and an outdoor ice-skating rink. For a small-town feel not far from downtown Washington, try **The Village at Shirlington** *(2700 S. Quincy St., 703-379-0007, off I-395, the Shirley Highway, accessible by car)*, for varied shops, restaurants, and movie theaters.

WHERE TO STAY

For luxury, minutes from downtown Washington, stay at **The Ritz-Carlton at Pentagon City ($$$)** *(1250 S. Hayes St., 703-415-5000 or 800-241-3333, www.ritzcarlton. com, Pentagon City Metro stop, Blue or Yellow Line).*

Featherbeds, marble baths, an indoor pool, fitness center, and elegant ambience are yours, with the convenience of the Metro at your front door. **The Virginian Suites (\$-\$\$)** *(1500 Arlington Blvd., 800-275-2866, www.virginiansuites.com, Rosslyn Metro stop, Blue or Orange Line)* is a family-friendly place with an outdoor pool and sundeck, complimentary coffee, newspapers, and shuttle to the Metro and a local grocery store. Studio-style and one-bedroom suites have fully equipped kitchens.

*Take Route 193, Exit 44 from the Beltway,
then go 4.5 miles west*

One of the most dramatic places in the Virginian sub-

urbs is **Great Falls Park** *(Great
Falls National Park, 9200 Old
Dominion Drive, www.nps.gov/
gwmp/grfa)*, where spectacular
waterfalls tumble 76 feet over
jagged rocks in the Potomac
River. Located 14 miles up the George Washington
Memorial Parkway from Washington, DC, this 800-
acre park is great for relaxation or hiking.

For out-of-the-ordinary Turkish food, music, and
atmosphere, visit **Kazan ($$)** *(6813 Redmond Dr., 703-
734-1960)*. Try Doner Kebab, their signature dish, of
marinated veal and lamb cooked over an open flame,
served in yogurt sauce over sautéed pita bread.

For upscale shopping, head to **Tysons Galleria** *(2001
International Drive, 703-827-7700, www.tysonsgalleria.
com)*, where Burberry, Cartier, Chanel, and Lacoste sit
side by side with Ann Taylor, J. Crew, Anthropologie,
and Coach. Another option is **Tysons Corner Center**
*(1961 Chain Bridge Rd., 703-847-7300, www.shop
tysons.com)*, where stores in every category from clothes
to eyewear, and beads to stationery abound.

Southern end of the George Washington Memorial
Parkway, 703-780-2000, www.mountvernon.org; use
Metro's Huntington stop on the Yellow Line, go to lower
level for Fairfax Connector Bus 101, 703-339-7200;
20-minute ride to the estate, or see chapter 7,
***Spirit Cruises (11)**, p. 164.*

Don't miss **Mount Vernon Estate and Gardens**
(www.mountvernon.org), located several miles south of
Old Town Alexandria. This was the home of George and
Martha Washington from 1759 until 1799. Tour the
mansion, outbuildings—including the slave quarters—
and the four-acre working Pioneer Farmer site. Two new
state-of-the-art facilities have recently opened highlighting various stages of Washington's life, including his
teenage years, military career, and his presidency.

MARYLAND SUBURBS— BETHESDA AND BEYOND

● SNAPSHOT ●

Maryland's suburbs are a collection of cities, towns, and districts that create an often-welcome change of pace from the DC dither. The area—largely Montgomery County, Maryland—includes public gardens, ethnic dining, art galleries, boutiques, entertainment choices, preserved farmland, parkland, and historic sites. In addition, it is home to the National Institutes of Health, the National Library of Medicine, and the National Naval Medical Center. Here, we focus on the best of Bethesda, with highlights from other communities.

PLACES TO SEE
Arts & Entertainment:

The Maryland suburbs have a variety of musical, theatrical, and dance programs. **Strathmore Hall Arts Center** *(10701 Rockville Pike, 301-530-5889, www.strathmore.org)* is a focal point for arts in the area, including art exhibitions, literary lectures, chamber music, folk music, jazz concert series, afternoon musical teas, performances for children, and outdoor  concerts. All programs are set in the Georgian-style mansion or in a 2,000-seat concert hall in the Music Center. Attend a performance at **Imagination Stage** *(4908 Auburn Ave., 301-280-1660, www.imagination stage.org)*, the largest multidisciplinary theater organization for young people in the Washington, DC, area. Literary adaptations, world premieres, and classic plays are featured.

PLACES TO EAT AND DRINK

Bethesda is a fun place to search for an affordable eatery away from the District. If you take the Red Line to the Bethesda Metro stop, you'll be able to walk to most places easily. One of the closest is the **Daily Grill ($$)** *(One Bethesda Metro Center, 301-656-6100, www.daily grill.com)*, serving traditional grill favorites at affordable prices. Family-friendly **Moongate ($)** *(4613 Willow Lane, 301-657-3740)*, offers Chinese food as good as it is plentiful. For hot and cold sandwiches, salads, and sides, try the popular **Booeymonger Bethesda ($)** *(4600 East West Highway, 301-718-9550, www.booeymonger.com)*.  Near the intersection of Bethesda and Woodmont Avenues, the **Barnes & Noble Café ($)** *(4801 Bethesda Ave., 301-986-1761, www.bn.com)* is fine for a light bite while you peruse newspapers, magazines, and books. For inexpensive, tasty Northern Indian food, go to **Delhi Dhaba Punjabi Grill ($)** *(7236 Woodmont Ave., 301-718-0008, www.delhidhaba.com)*. Lively **Jaleo ($-$$)** *(7271 Woodmont Ave., 301-913-0003, www.jaleo.com)* offers hot and cold tapas, plus weekly performances of Sevillanas dancers. **Austin Grill ($)** *(7278 Woodmont Ave., 301-656-1366, www.austingrill.com)* is a great place for Tex-Mex. You may have to wait for a table at the crowd-pleasing and unpretentious **Rio Grande Café ($)** *(4870 Bethesda Ave., 301-656-2981)*,  but the yummy food, large portions, and frozen drinks are worth it. **Café Deluxe ($)** *(4910 Elm St., 301-656-3131, www.cafedeluxe.com)* combines traditional comfort food with innovative new taste-tempters. In the mood for Mediterranean? You can't miss at **Tel-Aviv Café ($-$$)** *(4867 Cordell Ave., 301-718-9068, www.tel-aviv-cafe.com)* featuring a full-service martini bar and serving specialties like Moroccan game hen and Grecian moussaka.

If the weather permits, try the patio. Enjoy live music several nights a week.

WHERE TO SHOP

Art collectors will find galleries galore in Bethesda. **Creative Partners Gallery** *(4600 East-West Highway, 301-951-9441, www.creativepartnersart.com)* connects rising artists with new collectors. **Discovery Galleries, Ltd.** *(4840 Bethesda Ave., 301-913-9199,*  *www.discoverygalleries.com)* also showcases emerging artists. **Fraser Gallery** *(7700 Wisconsin Ave., Suite E, 301-718-9651, www.thefrasergallery.com)* was founded by award-winning photographer Catriona Fraser. **Gallery Neptune** *(4808 Auburn Ave., 301-716-0809, www.galleryneptune.com)*, an independent contemporary art gallery, is owned/operated by Bethesda artist Elyse Harrison. **Osuna Art** *(7200 Wisconsin Ave., 301-654-4500, www.osunaart.com)* offers antiques, modern art, old masters, and sculpture. **Ozmosis Gallery** *(7908 Woodmont Ave., 301-664-9662, www.ozmosisgallery.com)* presents original contemporary fine art with a focus on abstract works. If you're looking for trendy sportswear, shoes, or accessories, shop at **Luna** *(7232 Woodmont Ave., 301-656-1111, www.shopluna.com)*. For sophisticated mall shopping, **White Flint Mall** *(11301 Rockville Pike, 301-468-5777, www.shopwhiteflint.com; White Flint Metro stop, Red Line)*, has one of the best concentrations of upscale stores in one place, just a block away from the White Flint Metro station.

WHERE TO STAY

For those who prefer to stay far from the madding crowds, the **Doubletree Hotel-Bethesda ($-$$$)** *(8120 Wisconsin Ave., 301-652-2000 or 800-955-7359, http://doubletree.hilton.com)* fills the bill. Be pampered by its thoughtfully appointed rooms, fitness area, pool, and the **Notes Piano Bar and Grill**, open for breakfast, lunch, and dinner. The **Bethesda Marriott** *(5151 Pooks Hill Rd., 301-897-9400, http://marriott.com)* has 407 newly furnished rooms, an indoor and outdoor pool, exercise equipment, and two on-site restaurants.

● *to Bethesda; then take J2 or J3 bus
to Meadowbrook Lane*

The **Audubon Naturalist Society** *(8940 Jones Mill Road,
301-652-9188, www.audubonnaturalist.org)* focuses on
conserving biodiversity and protecting the wildlife habitat. Enjoy meandering through the wildflower meadow
and watch the aquatic life in the pond. If you're visiting
in May, bring the family to the Nature Fair that takes
place at the 40-acre nature sanctuary. **Clydes of Chevy
Chase** *(5441 Wisconsin Ave., 301-951-9600, www.
clydes.com)* re-creates the Orient Express in its main dining room. Downstairs, the "Race Bar" pays tribute to
the automobile. This popular eatery serves everything
from burgers to rotisserie chicken. Kids' menu is also
available.

● *to Friendship Heights or Bethesda;*
take Montgomery County Ride-on bus #29

A family-oriented, historic outdoor spot worth seeing is
Glen Echo Park *(7300 MacArthur Blvd., 301-634-2222,
www.glenechopark.org),* where everyone can ride a
restored 1921 Dentzel Carousel. Enjoy a puppet show
or a theatrical performance at Adventure Theatre. There
are art galleries and big-band and ballroom dances on
weekends held in the 1933 Spanish ballroom. The
Discovery Creek Children's Museum in the park is located
in a one-room schoolhouse and features innovative educational programs and exhibits focusing on the environ-
ment. The **Clara Barton National Historic Site** *(5801
Oxford Rd, 301-320-1410, www.nps.gov/clba),* housed
in a yellow warehouselike building, was originally used
as a storehouse for the American Red Cross in 1891. In
1897 the structure was remodeled when Clara Barton
moved there, and her furnishings and personal effects
are still on display.

By car take MacArthur Blvd. from DC to the end

One of the most beautiful places in Montgomery County is the **C&O Canal National Historic Park** *(11710 MacArthur Blvd., 301-767-3714, www.nps.gov/grfa)*, which offers scenic views of the **Great Falls** in Virginia. The National Park Service, which operates the park and the **Great Falls Tavern Visitor Center**, offers canal boat rides and interpretive programs. Enjoy a picnic as you hike the various trails through the forest and along the river. Rock

climbing and kayaking are also available for the very experienced. Arguably the prettiest restaurant in the Maryland suburbs is **Normandie Farm ($$)** *(10710 Falls Road, 301-983-8838, www.normandiefarm.com)*, where every meal is a special event. Combining a country atmosphere with French/continental cuisine, this antique-bedecked dining spot provides its now-famous popovers and raspberry preserves with every meal. Order the blackened stuffed filet of salmon, or beef Wellington. **Margery's Lounge**, adjacent to the lobby, provides live music on Friday and Saturday evenings. During warm weather, try the outdoor café.

● *to Wheaton*

Got a green thumb? Plan a trip to **Brookside Gardens**
*(Wheaton Regional Park, 1800 Glenallan Ave., 301-962-
1400, www.brooksidegardens.org)*, a 50-acre botanical
oasis with an azalea garden, a rose garden, a fragrance
garden, and two conservatories of tropical plants. There
is also a horticultural reference library and adult and
children's programs.

metro system
map